HIKING AND BACKPACKING

OUTDOOR PURSUITS SERIES

Eric Seaborg
Ellen Dudley

Human Kinetics

Library of Congress Cataloging-in-Publication Data

Seaborg, Eric, 1954-
   Hiking and backpacking / Eric Seaborg, Ellen Dudley.
     p.   cm.
   Includes bibliographical references (p.) and index.
   ISBN 0-87322-506-6
   1. Hiking. 2. Backpacking. I. Dudley, Ellen, 1938-
GV199.5.S43   1994
796.5'1--dc20   93-44075
                              CIP

ISBN: 0-87322-506-6

Series Editor: Holly Gilly; **Assistant Editors:** Sally Bayless, John Wentworth; **Copyeditor:** Merv Hendricks; **Proofreader:** Myla Smith; **Indexer:** Theresa J. Schaefer; **Production Director:** Ernie Noa; **Production Manager:** Kris Slamans; **Photo Editors:** Valerie Hall, Karen Maier; **Typesetter:** Ruby Zimmerman; **Text Designer:** Keith Blomberg; **Layout Artist:** Stuart Cartwright; **Cover Designer:** Jack Davis; **Photographer (cover):** © John Laptad/F-Stock; **Interior Art:** Thomas•Bradley Illustration and Design; **Printer:** Bang Printing

Human Kinetics books are available at special discounts for bulk purchase. Special editions or book excerpts can also be created to specification. For details, contact the Special Sales Manager at Human Kinetics.

Printed in the United States of America   10 9 8 7 6 5 4 3 2 1

Human Kinetics
P.O. Box 5076, Champaign, IL 61825-5076
1-800-747-4457

Canada: Human Kinetics, Box 24040, Windsor, ON N8Y 4Y9
1-800-465-7301 (in Canada only)

Europe: Human Kinetics, P.O. Box IW14, Leeds LS16 6TR, England
0532-781708

Australia: Human Kinetics, P.O. Box 80, Kingswood 5062, South Australia
618-374-0433

New Zealand: Human Kinetics, P.O. Box 105-231, Auckland 1
(09) 309-2259

CONTENTS

1

GOING HIKING AND BACKPACKING

The vast plateau of southeastern Utah stretched before us from horizon to horizon, its desert flatness punctuated by an occasional sandstone monolith. We felt we could walk forever through its silvery-green sagebrush and forest-green pinyon pines, with not an obstacle between us and a straight path to infinity.

Then suddenly the ground beneath our feet fell away into a yawning abyss. We stood on the south rim of a deep canyon. Our plateau continued from the north rim, just a few hundred yards away as the crow flies.

So into the chasm we walked, 2,000 feet (600 m) down along a boulder-strewn trail into a brand new world. Our limitless horizontal world tilted to an almost enclosed vertical one. Our new world consisted of the gurgling, waterfall-happy stream that had cut the gorge, cottonwood patriarchs on its banks, rock ledges rising stepwise, and red walls rising skyward, separated by a thin cobalt strip directly above.

Dudley/Seaborg © BACKPACKER Magazine

Dark Canyon reveals its colorful secrets to those willing to descend a steep, winding trail.

You would need as many words for red as the Inuit have for snow to describe all the shades of the rocks in the pillars and formations above us. The intensity of color even gave the light a sunset tint, as if we were looking through rose-colored glasses. For 3 days, as we made our way through the canyon, neither sight nor sound of another human intruded on this, our new world.

That dramatic change in worldview symbolizes the change in perspective that we always achieve when we go unfettered into the natural world. When we leave behind the world of concrete, automobiles, and television, we realize how artificial and constricting our day-to-day existence can be and how liberating it is to experience the natural world as it existed long before humans began adapting it for their comfort. We come back to the concrete world renewed, our cares left somewhere back on the trail.

Just as there are no roads to that canyon, there are no roads to a fresh perspective. You'll never see it through a windshield. To get there, you have to hike.

What Are Hiking and Backpacking?

Our dictionary defines *to hike* as "to go on an extended walk for pleasure or exercise." So *hiking* is simply a term for a specialized kind of walking. And backpacking means taking a hike carrying everything you need to stay out overnight.

To some people, the words have a forbidding mystique. Many are hesitant to venture forth, held back by the belief that hikers and backpackers have some arcane knowledge that enables them to find their way through the wilderness. Well, there is nothing so mysterious about walking on a trail. It can be mastered by anyone—and that's what this book is about.

Dudley/Seaborg

Anyone can master the skills required to venture onto trails like this one in Glacier National Park.

This book will tell you the things you need to know to get started. But it's not encyclopedic, and some experienced hikers could quibble that we've oversimplified a few issues. Much of our advice is based on the assumption that once you start hiking and backpacking you will read more in depth, talk to knowledgeable people, and learn from your own experiences. Indeed, you may find you've embarked on a lifelong project of learning and enjoyment.

Are Hiking and Backpacking for You?

Hikers have many reasons for their enthusiasm, but most can be summed up as experiencing nature, enjoying outdoor exercise, "getting away from it all," and the more-than-the-sum-of-the-parts feeling these add up to.

The Wonder of Nature

An elk herd rumbling across the trail into the pines; a scarlet tanager on a budding, spring-green tree; waves of snow-capped peaks—these are images you may never glimpse from a car. Walking is the only way to really see the country. By moving slowly, you feel a part of the land. Some take the opportunity to learn about the intricacies of the natural world, others just like to look at the views. Still others find hiking the best way to get to their favorite fishing holes or bird-watching spots.

Exercise

Hiking, especially up a steep incline, can provide the kind of steady, sustained exercise that many doctors recommend for health and weight control, without jarring your joints the way jogging can. It can be adapted to your fitness level, no matter what your age. It's a sport that has no mandatory retirement, growing with you as you grow older. The view of a waterfall or from a mountaintop gives you a much more satisfying feeling of accomplishment than does the view from a stationary bike. Getting there under your own power adds in some unexplainable way to your appreciation of the beauty.

Relaxation

One study found a 15-minute walk more effective than a tranquilizer. You can't get farther away from "it all" than the middle of a wilderness, and you can't buy a backpack big enough to carry your troubles. Out on the trail, your most important worries become "Is it going to rain?" and "When's dinner?"

Ironically, these primal cares provide perspective on what's important in your life. You have time to think—or to not think. In the vast world of forests and mountains, many of your cares look no larger than a hill of beans. You feel very small—and realize that's very good.

One of hiking's rewards: a dramatic perch overlooking the wilderness.

The Ineffable Sum

If this all sounds too cosmic, it's just another way of saying that hiking and backpacking are fun and make you feel good: feelings of awe at a vast landscape or at the intricate pattern on a butterfly's wing, feelings of peace and well-being. But trying to describe a feeling is like trying to describe the color red to a blind person.

DON'T TAKE OUR WORD FOR IT

"When you have worn out your shoes, the strength of the shoe leather has passed into the fiber of your body. I measure your health by the number of shoes and hats and clothes you have worn out. He is the richest man who pays the largest debt to his shoemaker."

—Ralph Waldo Emerson

"I go to my solitary woodland walks as the homesick return to their homes."

—Henry David Thoreau

"Climb the mountains and get their good tidings. Nature's peace will flow into you as the sunshine into the trees. The winds will blow their freshness into you, and the storms their energy, while cares will drop off like autumn leaves."

—John Muir

What is it about something as simple as walking that leads people to sing its praises? The only way to find out is to start hiking, to join the fraternity of kindred soles.

You won't be alone in taking up hiking. Hiking and backpacking have boomed in recent years (see the following sidebar). Hikers come in all shapes, sizes, and ages. The typical hiking club includes members from teenagers to octogenarians.

BACK TO BASICS

For millennia, walking was the way to get someplace if you didn't have a horse—and wilderness was something to be tamed.

In North America, wilderness began to take on an inherent value in the middle of the 19th century. The growing appreciation of nature became evident in the transcendentalist writings of Ralph Waldo Emerson and Henry David Thoreau and in the romantic landscapes of Albert Bierstadt and Frederick Church.

In 1876, the first association for the preservation and enjoyment of mountains, the Appalachian Mountain Club, was formed in New England. In 1890 John Muir and others founded the Sierra Club in San Francisco, not as the general environmental organization it is today but for the protection and opening for recreation of the Sierra Nevada. (Muir, whom we quote several times in this book, was a naturalist, writer, geologist, and popularizer of the outdoors; he is considered by many the father of Yosemite National Park.)

About the same time, the concept of preserving national parks in a pristine state for the enjoyment of current and future generations gained credence.

Still, heavy and ineffective camping and backpacking equipment kept difficult-to-reach places off-limits to all but the hardy few. The development of new materials coincided with increasing urbanization and the inevitable yearning to escape. For example, nylon replaced canvas in tents because it was a lighter and truly waterproof material. In the 1950s, an airline mechanic who was tired of heavy wooden pack frames welded a lighter metal frame, and his Kelty Pack company remains a leader.

The convergence of hiker-friendly materials and nature appreciation helped push people outdoors: After 1950, U.S. wilderness travel increased by 50% for every 5 years for a generation. The number of hikers and backpackers grew by 300% between 1965 and 1982.

Today, 165 million Americans consider "walking for pleasure" a significant leisure activity, 41 million dayhike, 13 million backpack, and the numbers continue to grow. The U.S. Forest Service projects that hiking and backpacking will grow by 30% in the 1990s.

This growth is not limited to the United States. In its 23 years, the European Ramblers' Association has grown to represent 5 million individuals in 25 countries.

Getting Started

Many of our first hikes were in Rock Creek Park, within the city limits of Washington, DC. But the wild kept calling us farther and farther, culminating in a yearlong expedition in which we mapped out the route of the American Discovery Trail, the country's first coast-to-coast trail.

Your hiking and backpacking career can begin as easily and grow with your ambitions. Many people progress from hiking to backpacking, but others find rewarding experiences without ever donning a full pack.

The best way to get started? Just mention to a hiker friend that you'd like to try the sport. Most hikers will jump at the chance to initiate a potential convert.

If you don't know a hiker, it's easy to find people who'll take you out on the trail. Just about every city has a hiking club. In Washington, DC, for example, seven clubs organize weekend hikes. All you need to take are your walking shoes, lunch, and minimal busfare or gas money.

How do you find a club? The weekend activities sections of newspapers often list hikes. A local outdoors equipment merchant may know of a club. You can write to the American Hiking Society for information on local clubs or to the Sierra Club (its local chapters generally include hikes in their activities). Also, American Volkssport Association chapters sponsor events—more likely to be walks on rural roads than hikes on woodland trails. Addresses for these organizations are in the appendix.

Once you've learned of a local club's hike, call the hike leader and explain that you're a novice. Ask questions about distance, hiking speed, difficulty, footwear (boots or lighter shoes), and whether beginners are welcome. Clubs and leaders have different hiking styles, ranging from slow wildflower walks to fast-paced, get-in-shape tune-ups. One group we hiked with introduced themselves before heading off, welcomed the beginners, and had a person assigned to the "sweep" position to ensure no one was left behind. Another club jumped off the bus without a word and practically ran up the mountain without a break. The trip leader, who wants a successful hike, usually will be straightforward about the group's attitude and goals.

When others on the hike find out that you're a novice, they'll often be eager to share their knowledge. Group hikes can relieve you of worries about getting lost, where to go, or what to bring. Groups offer social fun, but also impose more people between you and the solitude of the wilderness.

The next step may be to hike with your own small group. Find places close to home and choose first hikes that don't outdistance your strength and endurance. Some easy possibilities are flat old canal and railroad rights-of-way. Hike to a goal that offers a reward, such as a spot offering a nice view

© Nancy Hoyt Belcher/Photo Network

Hiking with a club is a great way to gain experience and meet others with similar interests.

or a waterfall.

To further your education, see if your local outdoors retailers sponsor free seminars.

If you like hiking and want to go on to backpacking, there are some easy intermediate steps. Some backcountry huts and lodges offer both beds and meals. You can lighten your pack by hiking to cabins and shelters that supply some equipment. Or try a commercial trip that offers inn-to-inn hiking, a hike leader, and a "sag wagon" to carry gear and tired hikers.

Your first overnight could be one for beginners with your local hiking club, guided by an experienced leader. If you can't find a club, look for professionally led trips. (If you just can't wait to learn about backpacking, you can sign up for a weeklong or monthlong course with a national outdoors school such as Outward Bound or the National Outdoor Leadership School.)

Once you've camped out with an organized group, you may be ready for your own weekend outing. One way to gain confidence in your equipment is to put your backpacking gear—and only that gear—in your car and pitch your tent at a campground where you can park next to your site. This way, you won't be isolated in the wilderness in case of problems. Then it's just a matter of piling on the experience. But we're getting a little ahead of ourselves. No matter what time of year you're reading this, get ready to call that hiking club, because outside of the snowbelt, most of them organize outings year-round.

But first you need to know what to take with you. That's what Chapter 2 is about.

NO EXCUSES: THE BILL IRWIN STORY

Getting started on an unfamiliar and challenging activity can be hard. You can always find reasons to put off that first conditioning walk or first trail hike.

If you find yourself coming up with excuses, think of Bill Irwin. He had the best reason in the world not to try hiking, especially not by himself out on a rough trail in the wilderness. He is blind.

Yet at age 50, with the help of his guide dog, Orient, this recovering alcoholic hiked the entire, 2,100-mile (3,380-km) Appalachian Trail.

He fell as many as 50 times a day. In his 8-month trip, he stretched ligaments, broke a rib, and smashed a finger. As he neared the finish, long after the other thru-hikers, he battled winds of 80 miles (128 km) an hour, temperatures in the teens, and snow up to his knees.

Why would anyone who couldn't even see the scenery undertake such a hike? Irwin says he "saw" the trail in "beautiful and exciting new ways."

Take the sound of the wind through the forest. It "rustled leaves, but it whistled through evergreen needles." It sounded different in spring's budding leaves than in summer's heavy vegetation.

Remember Irwin when you start hiking. Be open to how much your experiences can be enhanced by all your senses—how you can identify birds by sound as well as sight, how a waterfall sparkles in the sun but mists your cheeks.

When Irwin finished his trek, he had unique memories of the beauty— and he had a sense of accomplishment. You don't need to hike long distances to achieve the same sort of feeling because finishing any hike gives you a positive boost. The first time you complete a long hike, you'll be proud of yourself. And as you hike farther and higher, you'll have that sensation of accomplishment again and again.

2

EQUIPMENT YOU NEED FOR HIKING AND BACKPACKING

Hiking and backpacking are minimalist sports that provide a wonderful escape from the modern technological world. Walking is about as low-tech as you can get.

But luckily for you, the equipment has gone high tech while appearing deceptively simple. Thanks to miracle materials and innovative designs, you'll carry lighter loads and rough it more softly than the hikers of 20 or even 10 years ago.

Feet First

For both dayhiking and backpacking, your first concern is your feet because you won't do much walking without happy ones. In the 1970s it was almost a badge of honor to sport boots that weighed as much as your pack and took 3 years to break in. Hiking in tennis shoes was akin to challenging Everest without oxygen. But in these days when only wimps take oxygen up Everest, manufacturers are testing the limits of featherweight boots that take to your feet like slippers.

Hikers wear boots instead of shoes because boots provide two main kinds of protection: lateral support so you don't twist an ankle and a shield for your soles from the sharp rocks and pounding. Your need for this protection increases as you carry more weight and encounter rougher trails and terrain.

For your first hikes, you probably have a pair of sturdy walking shoes that will do the trick. Running shoes are not designed to give ankle support and so are not the best choice.

If you get hooked on hiking after a few outings, boots should be your first investment. If you plan on just dayhiking, you can buy light boots ($39-$115). But for an overnight backpack or for a week's walk cross-country off the trails, you'll need successively heavier boots ($49-$295). The amount of support you need is a matter of judgment and experience—some people simply have stronger ankles than others.

Why not simply buy the heaviest boot to be safe? Because 1 pound (0.45 kg) on your feet is as difficult to carry as 5 pounds (2.25 kg) on your back. If each step takes you 2 to 3 feet (0.6 to 0.91 m), there are about 2,000 steps in each mile (1.6 km). That's a lot of leg lifts to do with extra weight. And the heavier the boot, the stiffer it is, and the harder it tends to be to break in.

© KR Maier

Select boots that provide support and protection to match the terrain.

The Last Comes First

Tenderfoots often ask, "What's your favorite boot brand?" To which true masters can give only the Zenlike response, "It's the last that comes first." Or the only slightly more helpful, "My favorite boot is one that fits."

Each manufacturer builds its boots around a model of a foot called a "last," based on what it considers to be the "average" foot. Lasts vary in shape, just as human feet do—narrower in the toes and wider in the heels, roomier all around, higher in the arch. The key is to find the bootmaker who uses the last most like your foot. Your friends might rave about a favorite brand, but if it doesn't fit your feet the way it fits theirs, it won't work for you.

Finding the Right Boot

Take time to find the right boots. Unhappy feet have spoiled more hikes than any other problem.

TEST BOOT FIT CAREFULLY

1. Bring along both pairs of the socks you'll be hiking in to get a realistic idea of the fit.
2. A good store will have a steep ramp in its shoe department. Walk up the ramp to see if your heel slips in the boot you're trying on. Some slippage is inevitable, but more than a half inch (1.27 cm) is trouble. Walk down the ramp to see if your toes slip forward. If they hit the front of the boot, they'll turn black and blue when you descend steep hills. Kick the floor for a similar test.
3. Check for wiggle room for your toes. With the boot unlaced, you should be able to slide your foot forward and slip one finger (and only one) behind your heel.
4. Walk around the store. Flex, bend your knees, put your feet in the funny positions trail walking causes, and see if you feel any problems.
5. Remember that your feet probably will swell after hours of hiking. This is especially important to consider if you try on boots in winter when your feet are cold.
6. If you plan on using the boots for backpacking, put on a weighted pack when you try them on.

Look for quality workmanship and materials. Do the stitching and materials look solid? Will the boots keep your feet warm and dry? Details such as a one-piece tongue sewn over the front opening are good indicators of water-repellent design. The finer points may be hard to pick out, so talk to the salesperson.

Workers at reputable outdoors equipment stores usually use the gear themselves and are happy to share their knowledge. Beware the salesperson who tries to rush you into a decision. If in doubt, stick to well-known brands. (This is where ravings from friends *do* come in handy.)

COMFORT TIP Socks are almost as important as boots. Wearing two pairs at a time helps reduce friction on the feet. A thin polyester and nylon or spandex combination "liner" sock can help keep skin dry by wicking perspiration to the next layer. A heavier outer pair of socks should contain some combination of acrylic, wool, and stretch nylon and should be padded at the heel and the ball of the foot.

What to Wear in the Woods

You can start hiking and backpacking in clothes you already own, but as you get more serious about the sport you'll want to move away from natural fibers to synthetics with specialized performance capabilities.

At home, your clothes may be a fashion statement. But on the trail, your clothing is equipment with the important job of keeping you dry, warm, and comfortable. That can be difficult when you're exercising, especially in changeable weather.

Your body always emanates heat and moisture, but the amounts sky-rocket when you exercise. Evaporating sweat keeps you from overheating. Your clothing should hold in enough heat to keep you comfortably warm, but let excess heat and moisture escape.

The problem is keeping these factors balanced because hiking creates great swings in your heat production and heat loss. Sometimes you puff going uphill, you sweat copiously, your shirt gets saturated. Then you reach a ridge or peak where a sharp wind cools you off the moment it hits you. If the evaporation continues off that sweat-soaked shirt, you can quickly become chilled.

You might walk for several minutes on the cold ridge. Then as you head downhill, out of the wind, the temperature feels warmer. But because your body is not working very hard going downhill, you aren't generating much heat. The clothing you wore uphill may not be enough to keep you warm; the clothing you wore on the ridge may be too much.

Here are strategies to help you cope with changing conditions:

• *Keep in mind where you are going.* For example, as you climb into mountains, the weather becomes more extreme and the wind generally picks up. As a rule, the temperature drops about 3 degrees Fahrenheit (or 1.7 °C) for every thousand feet (305 m) of elevation gain, not counting wind chill. So you may need more clothes than you would at home or on a hike in the foothills.

• *Dress in layers.* Take them off going uphill to let the heat escape and put them back on going downhill when you're not pumping warm blood around as quickly. Have an extra layer for windswept mountain ridges.

• *Choose fabrics wisely.* Comfortable cotton is out because it absorbs water from sweat and rain. When wet, it not only loses its insulating power, it robs your body of heat. Wool is much better. Because it keeps its insulating value when wet, it was the mainstay of backcountry wear for years. But it is heavy, bulky, and itchy. Your best bets now are new synthetics.

Three-Layer System

One outdoors magazine says hikers no longer wear apparel; now they envelop themselves in "moisture-management clothing systems," also called the "three-layer system." The three layers are a synthetic knit against the skin, a pile pullover, and a "breathable" outer shell.

The skin layer is generally a high-tech knit polyester material such as polypropylene, Capilene, or Thermax—materials used to make lightweight tops, bottoms, gloves, and caps. These materials are hydrophobic—they wick sweat away from your body to an outer layer where it can evaporate. They are amazingly compact, light, and warm, even when wet.

The middle layer is a thicker polyester called pile or fleece. It comes as a pullover, jacket liner, or jacket and has a soft, fuzzy, terry cloth–like look. It, too, is warm for its weight, nonabsorbent, and wicks sweat farther from the body.

The third layer is a windproof, waterproof shell or jacket made of an innovative fabric that contains pores smaller than a water molecule but larger than a water vapor molecule. Thus, rainwater is repelled but water vapor from your body passes through—the garment "breathes." The best-known such fabric is Gore-Tex, which had the market practically to itself until competitors appeared recently.

The three-layer system keeps moving moisture away from your body. In colder weather, you can increase the thickness or number of layers.

The down jacket used to be a part of every backpacker's gear, but it has been largely supplanted by the wicking and warm-when-wet benefits of the synthetics. Down is lighter and less bulky than pile but worse than useless when wet. It's still an option, though, especially in cold and dry locales.

The three-layer system can keep you warm and comfortable on cold-weather hikes.

Below the Belt

In keeping warm, the trunk is the most important focus of attention, and for many hikers the kind of pants they wear seems like an afterthought. Even when the temperature drops to the 50s and 40s (about 10 °C) many hikers are most comfortable wearing shorts—especially going uphill. On a dayhike, you can pack lightweight polyester, nylon, coated nylon, or Gore-Tex pants to slip over your shorts when you reach windy ridges.

For chilly nights camping, synthetic knit long johns provide lots of warmth for their weight. Pile pants are also available.

If you're not ready to invest in specialized pants, any sturdy pair of pants will work well for your first backpacking trips. But those beloved cotton blue jeans, still commonly seen, are heavy and will be cold and slow to dry if they get wet.

Warm-Weather Dressing

In warm weather, clothing is naturally less of a worry. Shorts and a T-shirt may be all you need. A shirt made from a warm-weather synthetic such as CoolMax or Fieldsensor is good because it won't stay sweat-soaked as cotton will. Just remember, if you get wet in a rainstorm, you can be cold even if the temperature hasn't dropped. Take along a waterproof windbreaker or poncho, a lightweight synthetic knit top, and a knit hat to cope with unexpected contingencies.

In serious heat and sun, protect yourself by covering up with loose-fitting, light-colored, long-sleeved shirts and pants. A light-colored, broad-brimmed hat will shade your face and neck. Medical experts also recommend that you cover up when hiking in the woods—including wearing socks tucked into your pants—for protection from disease-bearing ticks (advice easier to give than to follow).

Rain Gear

The waterproofness and breathability of your clothing are obviously most important when it rains.

The popularity of breathable garments represents a consensus among outdoors equipment users that these garments are the best available option. They remain controversial, however. They have been known to fail in the field. The breathability of the fabric can be impaired by dirt and grime and overwhelmed by the heat and sweat generated by a backpacker hiking uphill. If perspiration condenses, it can no longer pass through the fabric's pores.

In an informal survey, hard-core backpackers reported lots of disappointment in Gore-Tex garments. But this disappointment seemed to be related to unmet high expectations. A Gore-Tex rainsuit can cost at least $200, and for that price people expect miracles.

As a beginner, you may want to start with a lower cost, lighter weight alternative such as a nonbreathable, polyurethane-coated nylon rainsuit ($50-$120) or poncho ($25-$35). (Don't even consider vinyl or plastic rainsuits for more than one-time, emergency use.) We've hiked with a load through sleet in shorts, shirt, and poncho and stayed adequately warm but not exactly dry.

© REI

Water repellency, ventilation, breathability, and weight are all important factors in selecting rain gear.

Here are additional considerations:

Don't expect to stay completely dry in an all-day soaking rain no matter what you wear. It often seems your choice is to get wet from either cold rain or warm sweat. If you unzip to let out the heat, water finds its way in. If you stay zipped, you sweat. Hiking in shorts helps let out the heat, and if you're warm enough while hiking, your skin dries quickly when you stop.

Ventilation in a garment is as important as breathability: If air laden with body moisture can find its way out without passing through a fabric, breathability is not an issue.

You generate a lot less heat when you hike with a daypack than with a full backpack. A breathable jacket may work fine on dayhikes but be overwhelmed during a backpack.

Ultimately, the choice is a matter of personal preference that can be answered only by experience.

SAFETY TIP An old mountain expression says, "If your feet are cold, put a hat on." Mountaineers know that in cold weather, lots of body heat escapes if your head is bare.

That makes a knit cap a key piece of equipment. You can take it off while climbing and put it on when resting on a chilly mountaintop. Backpackers often sleep in their caps.

A synthetic knit balaclava is our favorite headgear. Around your collar it's a neck gaiter; worn over your head it's a hat; and pulled up in front of your face it's a mask against frigid blasts.

Dayhiking Equipment

If you're taking a stroll in the park, all you need are walking shoes. But if you're headed out into any sort of wilderness, you need to take some basic gear and emergency essentials.

Be sure your daypack cargo includes gear to help you cope with unexpected weather changes or mishaps along the trail.

You'll be able to fit all you need easily into a **daypack** ($25-$100). The daypack need not be fancy—just a basic rucksack like students use for carrying books. A hipbelt makes the pack much more comfortable by taking the load off your shoulders, but it isn't absolutely necessary. For some summer hikes, you may even be able to fit everything into a fanny pack ($15-$30) or a lumbar pack ($60-$70)—small zippered bags that wrap around your middle.

On any hike, carry at least 1 quart (0.95 L) of **water** or other fluid. If you're going more than 5 miles (8 km), carry 2 quarts (1.9 L), and use your judgment and experience to adjust the amount according to distance, difficulty, and weather. (Don't drink out of streams; see "Water Treatment" later in this chapter.)

Take plenty of **food**—you'll earn the right to a hearty lunch. Also bring **snacks** to keep up a steady flow of energy. (See chapter 4 for trail foods.)

In case the weather worsens, you'll need **rain gear** and layers of **extra clothing**, which could be as compact and light as a synthetic knit top, coated nylon poncho or windbreaker, and balaclava or cap.

Even if you're hiking in a group with a leader, you should know the route and have your own **map** and **compass** in case you have to find your way back yourself. (Chapter 3 tells you how to use them.) A good **pocketknife** has many uses, from cutting moleskin to making repairs.

And what if a mishap occurs? The right gear, even something minor, could save your life. The problem could be as simple as having to find your way out after dark, which we've had to do more times than we'd like to admit. Get a lightweight **flashlight** at an outdoors equipment store and make sure your **batteries** are fresh. You won't be near an emergency room if someone gets hurt, so always keep a basic **first aid kit** with an instruction sheet in your pack. The sidebar on page 21 has suggested contents.

And for the remote possibility that you become lost or injured and have to bivouac overnight, take something to wrap up in, such as large plastic garbage bags, your poncho, or a paper-thin **space blanket**, which has a silver, heat-reflective side and a bright orange side that could help a search party spot you. To signal potential rescuers, pack a **whistle**, a **flare**, or both. Waterproof **matches** and a **firestarter** (such as a little tube of "fire ribbon") will enable you to light a flame for warmth or signaling. If you keep **emergency rations** such as high-energy food bars stashed in the bottom of your pack, they'll be there for this sort of situation, and if you bring **water-treatment pills** you can use water from a stream. By following the guidelines in this book, however, you should never end up bivouacking.

As you gain experience, you can adjust the equipment list according to hiking distance, terrain, weather, size of group, etc. But in the meantime, err on the side of caution. And keep in mind that we've discussed essentials only. You'll need some other important items like **sunblock, lip balm, sunglasses,** and **bug repellent**.

FIRST AID KIT CONTENTS

First aid instruction sheet

Antiseptic towelettes

Antibiotic ointment

Adhesive bandages

Adhesive tape

Gauze pads (large and small)

Butterfly closures

Roll gauze

Scissors (your knife may have good ones)

Tweezers

Needle

Triangular bandage

Elastic bandage

Aspirin/acetaminophen/ibuprofen

Safety pins

Moleskin and other footcare products

Iodine water-treatment tablets

Extractor (in snake country; see page 83)

Personal needs such as bee-sting allergy kit

Coins for phone calls

Paper and pencil for medical and rescue information

Possible Additions for Backpacking

(Talk to your doctor about some of these possibilities, especially for extended trips.)

Broad-spectrum prescription antibiotic

Prescription painkiller such as Tylenol with codeine

Dental repair kit

Benadryl (for bites and poison ivy/oak)

Antidiarrhea medicine

Laxative

Thermometer (with case)

Larger groups may want to share the weight of additional items, such as a splint.

Backpacking Equipment

Naturalist and Sierra Club founder John Muir filled the pockets of his greatcoat with oatmeal and tea and took to the mountains for days. Most of us are too soft for that approach. Fortunately for us softies, tremendous equipment innovations since the rise in the popularity of backpacking have made carrying a comfortable "home" easier than ever.

In backpacking, there's a built-in dynamic of balancing the comfort you can derive from the gear you carry against the difficulty of having to carry its weight. The expression "worth its weight in gold" can be shortened to simply "worth its weight": If you're going to need it, take it along. The trick is to know what you'll need and how to keep the weight of those items down.

Many backpackers obsess about weight, discarding the cover off a roll of adhesive tape, trimming the edges off maps, even cutting the handle off a toothbrush. Some of the tricks seem silly, but if your pack contains 72 items and you shave 1 ounce (28 g) off each one, your load will be 4-1/2 pounds (20.25 kg) lighter—the equivalent of two days of food.

In backpacking, as in economics, "need" has a tricky definition, balancing actual need versus desire. So weight versus need is a trade-off. Major equipment items almost everyone agrees the modern backpacker needs include backpack, tent, sleeping bag, sleeping pad, stove, and water-treatment system. And as you can see from the descriptions that follow, each item involves trade-offs.

Backpacks

You can carry much more gear in a backpack than in a daypack because a backpack has a rigid frame to distribute the pack's weight. The frame keeps the weight from hanging awkwardly from your shoulders by transferring it to your hips, where you can carry it much more comfortably and efficiently. So for any backpack an effective, padded hipbelt is a must.

There are two kinds of backpack frames: external and internal. An external frame is a rigid metal or plastic support on which the packbag hangs. An internal frame depends on metal stays inside the pack for rigidity. Each kind has strengths and weaknesses. Which is right for you depends on the kind of backpacking you plan to do and how much you want to pay. (See "At a Glance: Pack Frames.")

AT A GLANCE: PACK FRAMES

External frame

Best use: Trail travel

This frame holds the pack away from your body, which allows air to circulate and carry away some of the sweat from your back. But because it rigidly holds the load away from you, it doesn't move the weight as well with your motion as you might want. The frame can swing the weight away from your center of gravity and throw you off balance. This is not a problem on trails but is a disadvantage when hiking off-trail, scrambling over rocks, and crossing streams.

Cost: $120-$190 for 4,000 to 5,000 cubic inches (65,550 to 81,930 cu cm).

Internal frame

Best use: Off-trail travel

This frame hugs your body and moves with you. Its advantages are felt when mountain climbing, cross-country skiing, and hiking on rough terrain. The internal frame's flexible shape fits more easily into trunks and luggage racks and is less prone to damage by airline luggage handlers. But there are some disadvantages: This frame is harder to fit correctly to your body (a disadvantage to the novice, an advantage to the aficionado who can fine-tune it) and harder to load properly. It's harder to engineer one that can handle heavy loads as well as an external frame, which is probably why internal-frame packs are perhaps 50% more expensive than external-frame packs of similar quality.

Cost: $175-$300 for 4,500 to 6,000 cubic inches (73,740 to 98,320 cu cm).

You may find the external frame a better choice for a starter pack because of cost, ease of fit, and ease of loading. Also, you are likely to stay on trails until you are more experienced in the wilderness—which negates the internal frame's advantage in rough country.

But try on both kinds to see how they feel. Load each one and walk around the store. Can you get the weight onto your hips? Does it feel comfortable and look well made? Manufacturers finally are tailoring some models to the female physique, something to ask about if you can't find a good fit.

What size pack do you need? There are two schools of thought. Some believe the bigger the better. Others believe if you limit the size of your pack, you'll limit what you'll bring and lessen the weight.

The choice between an internal and an external frame pack depends on how you will use it and how the pack feels to you.

Larger packs weigh a bit more, but discipline in how much you pack is the real key to limiting weight. If you invest in a pack that can grow with your ability, you can progress to longer trips without buying a new pack.

Manufacturers provide the packbag's cargo capacity in terms of cubic inches. Keep in mind that your sleeping bag will be lashed to the outside of an external-frame pack, while it will be carried inside an internal-frame bag. Stuffed sleeping bags occupy between 800 and 1,500 cubic inches (13,104 to 24,580 cu cm), so subtract this amount from an internal's capacity when comparing it with an external.

According to *Backpacker* magazine, a capacity for internals of 4,500 to 6,000 cubic inches (73,740 to 98,320 cu cm) and for externals of 4,000 to 5,000 cubic inches (65,550 to 81,930 cu cm) is enough for a week's worth of gear—the size most backpackers will want.

Shelter

What could be more romantic than sleeping out under the twinkling stars, watching the moon track across the sky? Watching the clouds blow across the moon, feeling the rain pelting your face, shivering as rainwater soaks into your sleeping bag? Enough said. Unless you're absolutely sure it's not going to rain, you'll need some shelter with you.

Tent or Tarp?

The lightest protection is a tarp system, which if rigged properly will keep you dry in moderately inclement weather. But we recommend a tent for beginners because it is easier to use and more reliable. Anyone can put up a tent, but rigging a tarp well takes experience. A tent is worth its weight because it eliminates the possibility of getting soaked, which can extinguish any smoldering desire for backpacking and can even put you in danger. A tent is much more expensive, but you can rent one until you decide if you want to buy. Decent tarps are getting hard to find—and the cheap plastic you will be tempted to buy will rip so soon it's not worth carrying.

A tent is also better because it cuts the wind and holds in your body heat (it can be 10 to 20 degrees warmer than outside), it keeps out biting insects, and it provides privacy when car camping.

Choosing a Tent

If you're going to do anything more rigorous than summer camping in mild climes, you'll need a tent rated as "three-season" (which will cost $130-$340 for a two-person size). Tents rated "two-season" (or "one-season" or "summer") are light and cool, designed more for keeping out the bugs than the chill. And "four-season" or "mountaineering" tents are overkill for a beginner.

You can get wet two ways when you're catching up on your sleep: from precipitation and from condensation. Your breath and skin constantly give

Dudley/Seaborg © BACKPACKER Magazine

A tent is your ticket to a comfortable overnight in a pristine spot.

Tent Types

Manufacturers often blur distinctions and mix characteristics to form hybrids, trying to combine the best features of different tent shapes.

A-Frame

This traditional design's sloping walls shed rain and wind well but provide little head or sitting room within. The pure A-frame is not often seen anymore, but modified versions still serve well.

Dome

The almost straight walls of domes and modified domes provide the most interior space of any design. They are great for sitting up in, dressing in, waiting out storms, and winter camping when you'll spend more time inside. But the space (and weight) may be more than you need if you're sure you'll only use it for sleeping.

Tunnel (Hoop)

Tunnels can provide some of the straight-wall features domes offer in interior space, but they also can be tapered at the foot where space is less important. They can be some of the lightest tents but are a tight fit.

Vestibule

A tent of any shape can have extra space sheltered by the fly for cooking, eating, and storing gear. This is a weight-efficient way to increase usable space.

Freestanding

Tents of any shape also can be designed to be self-supporting without stakes. This feature can be especially helpful in rocky ground, but you still have to anchor them with stakes or weight to prevent a wind gust from blowing them away.

off water vapor that can condense on tent walls and drip onto your sleeping bags and clothes. That's why standard tent construction involves two layers—an inner, nonwaterproof layer and a separate, waterproof rain fly. The fly spreads like a canopy over the tent without touching it, leaving a space between. Vapor from your body rises through the tent wall and leaves via the space beneath the fly.

Tents are rated according to the number of people they hold, such as two-person or three-person. But they are rated for a tight fit, and the perceived size shrinks in relation to the amount of time you spend inside. Two people waiting out a daylong storm will find a small two-person tent claustrophobic. You might have to spend the whole time lying down; in a larger tent you could sit up and move around.

Other considerations on size: If your sleeping bag touches the tent walls, condensation will make it soggy. You can't cram people into a tent like a phone booth. Some people like to bring their gear into the tent or vestibule. (Note: Food should always be left outside.)

Tents come in a bewildering array of shapes, including domes, A-frames, tunnels, and hybrids. Climb in and try a tent on for fit. The shape that's right for you depends on personal preference and how you'll use it.

Good tents come with waterproof floors and "tub construction" (waterproof material up the sides that keeps out water running on the ground). But because the floor is usually the first thing to wear out, many backpackers protect their investment by placing a nylon or plastic ground cloth or space blanket under the tent to protect it from abrasion, rocks, and roots. (A ground cloth's edges should not protrude past the tent's edges or water may collect under your tent.)

Sleeping Bags

A sleeping bag's job description is simple: to hold in your body heat to keep you comfortable on cold nights.

The standard sleeping bag for backpackers is shaped like a mummy. Cut tight around your feet, it expands in a V to your shoulders, then forms a hood around your head. Its zipper generally goes half to three-quarters of the way down one side. A tighter fit is more efficient because you heat less air space, but it provides less rolling room and is less comfortable. Backpackers avoid rectangular shapes that unzip on two sides because they aren't adequately warm, weight efficient, or space efficient.

Your two main decisions in picking a sleeping bag are choosing its insulation material and its temperature rating.

Insulation Material

Bags are filled with either goose down or a synthetic down imitator. The synthetics are sold under a variety of brand names, most of which incorporate some form of "fill," "loft," or "lite." Not all synthetics are equal. "Continuous filament" synthetics cost more and work better.

Temperature Rating

Manufacturers rate each bag model according to a theoretical coldest temperature at which the bag will keep you comfortable. Use these ratings as rough estimates only because manufacturers do not follow standardized guidelines. But the rating and the manufacturers' reputations are about all you have to go on.

How warm a bag you need depends on your personal heat-generating characteristics and how you will use the bag. If you still pile blankets on your bed in August, you "sleep colder" than most people and should add 10 to 20 degrees (about 8 °C) to the temperature rating. If you don't get out the blankets until January, you "sleep warm" and don't need as thick a bag.

Will you use the bag in the Sierra Nevada in winter or in Florida in March? If you know where you'll be going, check hiking guides and

---

AT A GLANCE: SLEEPING BAG FILLS

Cost
(for bag rated to 20 °F, –7 °C)

Goose Down $160-$275

Advantages: Lightest known insulator
Most compactible
Lasts up to three times longer
Greater "comfort range" (not as hot
and clammy on warmer nights)

Disadvantages: Useless when wet
Dries very slowly
More expensive initially

Synthetics $100-$200

Advantages: Retains some insulating power
when wet
Dries more readily
Easier care

Disadvantages: Heavier
Bulkier

almanacs for weather conditions you're likely to encounter. You can rent or borrow bags to see how they agree with you. Or you can pick a temperature rating—20 degrees (–7 °C) is a reasonable one for an average sleeper—and figure that you won't use it in conditions much worse than that.

You can extend the bag's temperature range by wearing dry (not sweaty) clothes to bed. Sleeping with a cap or balaclava on adds greatly to your warmth. You can also add a liner to lower the temperature range. For warmweather camping, for instance summer at the beach in Virginia, simply carry a sheet and light thermal blanket.

Don't be shy about shaking a bag out on the floor of the store and crawling inside to check it for fit and feel. Is it long enough? Too long? Roomy? Does it have marks of quality workmanship such as an insulating strip behind the zipper and a well-shaped hood with drawstring? (Keep in mind that two mummy bags can be zipped together to make one double bag if you buy them with zippers on opposite sides.)

CONSUMER TIP   The stuff sack that comes with a sleeping bag is often too small. You'll never compress your bag as much as they did at the factory. Buy a larger stuff sack that you can line with a plastic bag for waterproofing.

Sleeping Pads

One obvious problem is that the weight of your body compresses the fill of the sleeping bag under you to practically nothing. You can actually lose more heat to the ground than to the air around you. That's why backpackers also carry a sleeping pad. A good pad also smooths out those bumps, roots, and rocks that seem to grow by the hour as you toss and turn on them.

There are two basic types of sleeping pads: closed-cell foam and a selfinflating mattress filled with an open-cell foam. At the turn of a valve, the mattress pads inflate to about 1-1/2 inches (3.81 cm) thick. (These selfinflating mattresses are not to be confused with beach or summer campstyle air mattresses, which are not recommended for backcountry use because of weight, bulk, and a tendency to puncture.)

AT A GLANCE: SLEEPING PADS

		Cost (3/4-length)
Self-Inflating		$35-$82
Advantages:	Twice the insulating value	
	Much more comfortable	
	Less bulky to carry	
Disadvantages:	Two to three times heavier	
	More expensive	
	Can puncture	
	(carry tape or repair kit)	
Closed-Cell Foam		$10-$18
Advantages:	Lighter	
	Less expensive	
	Virtually indestructible	
	(for turning rocks into chairs around camp)	
Disadvantages:	Not as insulating	
	Not as comfortable	
	Bulkier	

Rent or borrow each type for a field test. If that's not possible, lie on them on the store floor with a pocketknife or other object underneath to simulate the experience of lying on bumpy ground. The mattresses appear an extravagance, but most people wouldn't dream of giving them up after trying them.

COMFORT TIP   Improvise the other component for a good night's sleep—a pillow—by wrapping clothes in a stuff sack or fleece pullover.

Stoves

A cookstove has become standard equipment for the backpacker for several reasons not immediately apparent to the newcomer. Why would anyone carry the extra weight when there's often plenty of wood around to burn? First, fires are prohibited in many of the best places to camp, including many national parks. There are several reasons: the proliferation of ugly fire rings;

Stove Types

White Gas

White gas is a pure form of gasoline that provides a very hot flame. You carry it as a liquid, but starting the stove involves a priming procedure to pressurize the fuel, which can lead to frightening (although usually momentary) flare-ups. The flame is appreciably hotter than canister or alcohol stoves—which means it boils your water more quickly but can be too hot for a good simmer. White gas is easy enough to find in the United States and Canada as Coleman fuel, Blazo, or other brands, but harder to find in other countries. (Cost: $37-$80.)

© KR Maier

© KR Maier

Kerosene

Kerosene is another liquid fuel that relies on a priming procedure, but it is harder to light and work with. It burns with a hot flame. Kerosene stoves are not commonly used except by those capitalizing on their main virtue— the wide availability of the fuel, even in the Third World. (Cost: $50-$80.)

© KR Maier

Multifuel

Multifuel stoves can be adapted to burn two or more petroleum-based liquid fuels, such as white gas, automobile gas, or kerosene. They are good for the far-ranging traveler. (Cost: $57-$150.)

Fuel for **alcohol stoves** is less volatile, is not petroleum-based, and requires no priming, but the flame is not nearly as hot as with other liquid fuels. These stoves are uncommon except in Scandinavia. (Cost: $25-$85.)

Canister

Canister types burn pressurized gas: butane or a butane/propane blend. They are convenient—just turn a knob to light the flame and cook. The flame is not as hot as white gas but is fully adjustable to a true simmer. The drawback of butane is that its performance drops with the temperature. Below

© KR Maier

freezing, butane may not work at all, while blended fuel works in temperatures down to the teens. (At higher altitudes, however, canister stoves actually work at lower temperatures with hotter flames.) Other drawbacks: Spent canisters stink and must be packed out (tape over the hole), and canisters cost significantly more per BTU than white gas. Fuel canisters can be found in most (but not all) camping stores in the United States and Canada and are common in western Europe. (Cost: $30-$51.)

the removal of wood that would otherwise enrich the soil; fire danger; and irresponsible fuel gathering, such as by stripping trees. Even where fires are allowed, many backpackers shun them to lessen their impact on the beautiful places they visit, leaving behind as little trace as possible.

Second, cooking on a stove is easier, faster and has other practical advantages: no smoke inhalation, no ashes in your food, no blackened pots, no sparks burning holes in clothes and equipment, no firewood gathering, and no worries about kindling wet wood after a storm. When you drag into camp cold and wet, you need to quickly get warm food into your body instead of wandering around looking for dry wood. Your clothes, sleeping bag, tent, and hot food are much more important survival tools than a fire.

Backpacking stoves boil down to several broad categories according to the kind of fuels they burn.

A factor to consider is the availability of the fuel where you'll be backpacking. For safety reasons, you can't take fuels like white gas and butane on public transportation.

Water Treatment

Years ago hikers tasted every sparkling stream they passed. Unfortunately, that spontaneous pleasure is no longer safe because of a protozoan that has found its way into streams across the country. *Giardia lamblia* can cause severe diarrhea, flatulence, abdominal bloating, weakness, and malaise.

On a dayhike you can carry all the water you'll need. For a backpack, you'll need to purify any water you can't be sure of. And we doubt you can ever be sure: We've seen a doe defecating in a creek, a dead moose in a stream, and sheep grazing on the ridges above our high altitude campsite.

The most reliable treatment is to boil the water briskly, which will kill not only *Giardia* but also bacteria and viruses. *Giardia* will die at a boil, but researchers recommend 10 minutes at sea level for other biological contaminants. At high altitude, water boils at a lower temperature, so it should be boiled longer, perhaps 1 minute per thousand feet (305 m). Still, few people boil all their water on an extended backpack because it takes too much time and uses too much fuel. It also leaves the water warm and flat tasting.

The easiest treatment is to add iodine (which comes in tablets, crystals, and liquid). Iodine kills bacteria, viruses, and *Giardia*. In cold, murky, or discolored water you need to double the dose and allow much more time for it to work. (But don't keep popping in pills—iodine is safe for humans in the recommended doses but kills pathogens because it's a poison.) Pregnant women and people with thyroid conditions should consult their physicians before using it. A disadvantage is that it gives your water the flavor of a doctor's office. The pills have a limited shelf life. Some experts recommend buying a new supply annually. (Iodine pills cost about $5 for a bottle that will treat 50 quarts or liters of clear water or 25 quarts or liters of turbid water.)

Chlorine-based treatment is not reliable.

COMFORT TIP   Powdered flavorings can mask the taste of iodine, but add them only after the iodine has had time to work. Added too soon, they interfere with iodine's effectiveness.

Many backpackers carry high-tech water filters ($26-$220). Key characteristics for judging a filter are the size of the particles it removes and its ease of use. *Giardia*, your largest nemesis, can be kept at bay with a 4-micron filter. Bacteria require a 2-micron filter. Viruses are so small that no practical filter can remove them, but they are not a worry unless you'll be traveling in the Third World. Even the 2-micron size is small enough to clog quickly, so many filters designed to eliminate bacteria and viruses also incorporate iodine treatment. No agency regulates filter makers, so you're

Sam Carlson © BACKPACKER Magazine

Water filters are a high-tech way to provide safe drinking water.

at the mercy of manufacturers and equipment reviews when it comes to judging their claims.

Factors affecting ease of use include the rate at which it delivers clean water, the ease of cleaning the filter (they all clog eventually), whether the filter can be cleaned in the field, and how convenient you find the tubing setup. A prefilter takes out the largest particles to keep the main filter running freely longer.

Some medical authorities say the danger from *Giardia* has been over-blown. People vary in susceptibility, and up to half of those infected exhibit no symptoms. That may explain why many people drink untreated water or treat their water infrequently with no apparent ill effects.

COMFORT TIP   Take along a collapsible "dirty water" jug that you can dip into the source and then carry to a comfortable place to perform the filtering. This also lets particulates settle and keeps them out of your filter.

CUTTING THE COST OF GEAR

A complete outfit of backpacking gear can easily cost $1,000, a sum you won't want to spend before sampling the activity to see if it's for you.

Fortunately, there are several ways to cut your start-up costs. Most of the high-ticket items can be rented. You also can borrow equipment or go with friends and share their equipment. Or you can go on an organized trip where the outfitter supplies equipment.

If you get bitten by the backpacking bug, then assemble your arsenal a piece at a time, starting with your boots. The gear in an army surplus store may be not high-tech, but it may be serviceable. Be careful, though. Good gear is expensive for a reason, and used brand name equipment will often last better than new, but cheap alternatives. You can usually see the amount of wear on used equipment such as packs. Hold sleeping bags up to the light; where the light comes through, the fill has shifted and left a "cold spot." Set up tents, simulate a rainstorm with a hose, and look for leaks (leaky seams can be sealed). Avoid used water filters, because you can't see inside where it counts.

Look for secondhand items through bulletin boards at stores, hiking club newsletters and contacts, and end-of-season sales of rental equip-ment. Ask your friends who backpack if they have old equipment they've replaced. If you're really lucky, you'll stumble on a gear freak addicted to the latest innovation who has a closetful of "outmoded" equipment.

What Else Do I Need?

The items described in this chapter comprise the specialized gear for backpacking. Of course, you'll also need to take other items of daily life. You can find many of them around the house. For example, while specialized backpacking cooksets are available, you probably have a lightweight pot around the kitchen. For water bottles, you can use plastic soda bottles, although they're more fragile than standard water bottles. For a pack cover, try a plastic garbage bag.

Think carefully about what you need. You won't want to carry a new outfit for every day; in fact, you'll learn that wearing the same clothes over and over again is not so bad, at least not when your companions' clothes aren't fresh either! On the other hand, if some of your clothes get wet, you need spares.

The best way to stay organized and make sure you have everything is to work from a checklist. The sidebar on pages 38-39 provides one for you. Actually, it contains more than you would ever take on a single trip because your equipment will vary from trip to trip, depending on the weather, season, trip length, and priorities. One trip may be for photography and on another you may pack light and cover ground. Flashlights will get more use on a fall or winter trip but insect repellent may not be needed at all.

Most of the items on the checklist are obvious. But here are a few that need a little explanation:

• Most hikers are converts to Swiss Army knives, which are made by Victorinox and Wenger. The model we use has both large and small blades, can opener/screwdriver, bottle opener/screwdriver, corkscrew, and leather punch/awl (which we'd like to trade for a Phillips screwdriver). The only other tool we recommend is a pair of scissors; knives that include the kitchen sink are too heavy.

• You'll need a 50-foot (15-m) length of rope to hang your food properly in bear country, but bring more. Bring the 1/8-inch (0.32-cm) diameter, parachute-cord type. It can be used to tie things to your pack (tents, socks, anything you want to dry); for repairs; to tie a tent fly to rocks when stakes won't go in the ground; as a spare bootlace; as a clothesline; and for uses you can't imagine until something breaks. We used some once to tie on a boot sole that had come unglued.

• A headlamp instead of an ordinary flashlight leaves both hands free for cooking, cleaning up, or reading while nestled in your sleeping bag.

BACKPACKING CHECKLIST

Backpack
Pack rain cover

Clothing

Boots
Socks
Underwear
Shorts
Long pants
Knit synthetic top
Knit synthetic bottom
Short-sleeved/long-sleeved shirts
Pullover/sweater
Jacket/parka/windbreaker
Rain gear (poncho, rain
  pants/chaps, gaiters, parka)
Sun hat/visor
Gloves/mittens
Warm hat

Sleeping Equipment

Tent with fly
Tent poles
Tent stakes
Ground cloth/space blanket
Sleeping bag (with stuff sack and
  plastic bag)
Sleeping pad

Food

____ Breakfasts
____ Lunches
____ Dinners
Condiments (margarine, spices,
  flavor packets)
Hot drinks
Emergency food

Cooking Equipment

Water bottles
Stove
Fuel bottle (full) or gas
  cartridge(s)
Pouring spout or funnel for
  fuel (if necessary)
Windshield for stove
Cooking pot(s)
Frying pan (if necessary)
Cup/mug
Plate/bowl
Spoon
Matches (at least some
  waterproof)
Water filter/water-treatment
  tablets
Can opener (if necessary)
Dish scrubber

Other Essentials

First aid kit, including
  foot-care items
Maps
Compass
Flashlight
Spare flashlight batteries
  and bulb
Repair kit: needle and polyester
  or nylon thread (can sometimes use waxed dental
  floss), rubber bands, ripstop
  or duct tape, tent pole sleeve,
  nylon cord, wire, spare pack
  parts like clevis pins, safety
  pins, glue, patch kit for selfinflating mattress

Sunglasses
Sunscreen
Lip balm
Insect repellent
Nylon rope
Pocketknife
Toilet paper
Plastic trowel
Pen and paper
Plastic bags/stuff sacks for trash,
 waterproofing, organizing,
 hanging food
Candle/fire starter
Whistle/signal mirror/smoke
 bomb/flares
Biodegradable soap (does you
 and dishes)
Toothbrush and toothpaste/
 baking soda and dental floss
Bandannas
Scissors (if not in first aid kit or
 on knife)
Watch

Miscellaneous Desirables

Walking stick/ski pole
Guidebook (or just relevant
 pages)
Comb
Field guides
Paperback book
Thermometer
Swimsuit
Towel
Wash cloth/Handiwipes/
 moistened wipes
Camp shoes
Binoculars
Magnifying glass
Photography equipment
Playing cards
"Dirty water" container
Spare prescription glasses

© KR Maier

A headlamp frees both hands for cooking, reading, and other tasks.

• Shoes to wear around camp relax your feet after a hard day in boots and help lessen soil compaction and tread damage around your campsite. A pair of running shoes will do, but alternatives like "aqua shoes," which have breathable stretch mesh on top and waffle traction soles (good for fording streams), weigh only 10 ounces (280 g).

• A hiking staff has many uses: for balance on rocky trails and stream crossings, to involve arm muscles and take some of the load off the legs, to ward off vegetation on overgrown trails, as a pole for a makeshift shelter, and as a support to hold your pack up as a backrest. You can pick up a sturdy branch you find in the woods for free, but a lighter option is the ski pole–type staff that telescopes from 2 feet (0.6 m) for storage and going uphill to 5 feet (1.5 m) for deep water and going downhill. Some even double as a camera monopod.

• Dips in streams or lakes are refreshing, but regular towels are bulky, heavy, and slow to dry. A pile pullover is a great substitute, but a camp towel of soft, absorbent viscose wrings 92% dry and can be used as a potholder and sponge. A kitchen-towel-size swatch weighs 1.5 ounces (42 g); a small bath-towel size weighs 5 ounces (140 g).

• Prowl the aisles of a backpacking store for other innovations: "no rinse" cleansers, unbreakable acrylic 1/2-ounce (14 g) mirrors, pants with zip-off legs that convert to shorts, and backpacks with a zip-off fanny pack for dayhiking from a base camp.

Think about every item. For example, will you need more than one pot? You may even need to visualize or write down the cooking sequence to figure out exactly what you need. Will you need a pot holder or pot grabber (or will a bandanna do)? What about washing the dishes?

Be creative. For instance, a bandanna can be used as a pot holder, headband, sling, neck warmer, hat, napkin, dishwasher, washcloth, and towel (hang it on your pack to dry). A plastic garbage bag can be a poncho, pack cover, and sit-upon in wet weather. It's also possible to outsmart yourself. For instance, we once left our pack rain covers at home because we thought our ponchos would cover our packs. That worked fine as long as we were wearing our packs. When we took them off, however, our ponchos couldn't be two places at once.

Now that you know what you need, let's talk about how to use it.

3

HIKING AND BACKPACKING CORRECTLY

Early each spring, more than 1,200 pack-laden hopefuls start north from Springer Mountain in Georgia. Their goal is Mt. Katahdin in Maine, at the other end of the Appalachian Trail. These people are committed—they've made a big investment in gear and have arranged to leave their homes for 5 to 6 months.

And yet a quarter of them will drop out after just 30 miles (48 km), at the first place the trail crosses a road. Incredibly, they simply didn't know what they were getting themselves into. Their failure is all the more surprising because there is nothing so mysterious about hiking and backpacking—the skills mostly boil down to experience and common sense.

It doesn't take much skill to pick up one foot and put it in front of the other. But before you head off to tread terra incognita, there are a few things you need to know. The skills aren't related to coordination, like hitting a baseball, but to knowledge and attitude.

First, a few words about attitude.

Minimizing Your Impact

The hiker's and backpacker's mantras are "If you pack it in, pack it out" and "Leave only footprints, take only memories." Both are shorthand for saying that you are a visitor to the backcountry and should have as little impact on it as possible.

Dozens, hundreds, even thousands of people may use the trail you're on each year. What if each one did a seemingly innocuous act—picking a flower, breaking a branch from a tree, tossing out a gum wrapper?

Leave no litter, no matter how small. Even biodegradables like orange and banana peels should be packed out because they take months to decompose, long enough certainly for others to come along and see the debris. Always ask yourself, If someone else comes by, in a few minutes or in a few months, will they be able to tell I was there?

Walk quietly so others in the area can savor the pure delight of the sounds of nature—birds singing, branches rustling in the wind. Save the shouting for emergencies.

When you camp, choose an unobtrusive site, and leave no evidence of your passing.

Backcountry Sanitation

One of your most important responsibilities in the backcountry is to avoid polluting it—and this is especially true of water. Many streams and lakes have been fouled by backpackers and hikers who practiced poor sanitation.

The primary rule is to introduce *nothing*—no soap, no food, no bodily waste—into any stream, lake, water, or watercourse. (By "watercourse" we mean a place where water collects or runs after a rain. If you pollute such a spot, runoff from the next rain will carry your contamination directly to a stream.)

Urine does not pose a health hazard, so just use common courtesy. For other bodily needs, follow these guidelines.

PRACTICE PROPER SANITATION

1. Carry a plastic bag for packing out toilet paper, tampons, and sanitary napkins.
2. Trailheads and campsites sometimes have outhouses; use these whenever you can (and only for their intended use—don't drop your litter in the hole).
3. When there's no outhouse nearby, first select a site far from any possible water contamination. Recommendations vary from as little as 30 or 50 feet (9 to 15 m) to as much as 300 to 600 feet (91 to 183 m) away. Given the fact that some streams have become polluted, people obviously aren't going far enough. It shouldn't be too much trouble to get at least 200 feet (61 m) from any watercourse, so go as far as you reasonably can. Avoid sites that someone could conceivably want for a campsite one day. (If you're camping in a popular area, walk up the trail at least a quarter mile [0.4 km], then turn off into the woods, to diffuse the pollutants over a greater area.)

   Then dig a hole 4 to 8 inches (10 to 20 cm) deep. Don't dig deeper because this is the soil zone where decomposition takes place. If you carry a light plastic trowel as part of your gear, you'll find it much easier to comply with proper practices.

   Ideally, you should pack your toilet paper out with you. Some people burn the paper, but that's risky because hikers have actually started forest fires this way. If you burn, be careful and make sure the fire is out completely. Don't burn toilet paper if the spot contains duff, dried leaves, or other flammables. The hardiest purists use no toilet paper and say that natural alternatives work just fine.

   Finally, cover feces well with dirt.
4. Leave an open water bottle and soap handy so you can wash your hands when you return to the trail or campsite.

Do all your washing (including brushing your teeth) at least 50 feet (15 m) from any watercourse. Fill a pot with water and take it away from a stream or lake to wash dishes, clothes, or yourself. If you use soap, make it biodegradable.

The importance of proper sanitation cannot be overemphasized. Many wilderness streams and lakes have been contaminated with *Giardia* and bacteria. If the trend continues, even worse pathogens, such as hepatitis, could be introduced.

The northern end of the Appalachian Trail: Mt. Katahdin in Maine.

TRAIL MANNERS

The outdoors world has its own simple code of etiquette:

Courtesy and friendliness are hallmarks of the hiking world, so greet those you meet along the trail.

Stay on the trail. Don't walk around a muddy spot to spare your boots. When hikers do this, the trail enlarges to become an unsightly scar in the woodlands.

Never take shortcuts, and don't hike on closed trails.

Give uphill hikers the right of way. If you're on a combination hiking and riding trail, step aside and remain still to let horses pass unspooked.

Living With Wildlife

Never feed any animals, even accidentally by dropping food at your campsite or tossing biodegradable litter into the woods. Feeding wild animals teaches them to associate humans with food, which encourages them to become pests, beggars, and thieves, a real problem in bear country. It's also hazardous to animal health. They are as happy to eat junk food as we are, but straying from the diet that nature intended can lead them to sickness and death.

Breaking In Your Boots

A Chinese proverb says, "To forget your troubles, wear tight shoes." When every step hurts, even the most beautiful trail becomes a perverse torture. The cares of the world slip away when you're out hiking under the sky, but only if you've broken in your boots well enough to avoid blisters and sore feet. Fortunately, today's lightweight boots need little breaking in.

BREAK IN BOOTS CAREFULLY

1. Adjust boots to your feet—and vice versa—by wearing them around the house, to the store, or anyplace else where you can change out of them if your feet start to hurt.
2. Gradually lengthen the amount of time you wear them.
3. Identify potential trouble spots on your feet and protect them. Blisters, caused by the heat of friction, can be prevented by reducing the rubbing by covering the skin with adhesive tape, moleskin, or even duct tape.

Your feet will let you know when your boots are ready for the trail. But even broken-in boots may not always be trouble free. Boots shrink and stiffen after being soaked in the rain. Your feet change size according to the temperature and the load you're carrying. Even a faster-than-normal pace can cause unexpected irritation.

So always take along moleskin and tape and give your feet TLC at the first sign of a hot spot, pinch, or any other discomfort. If you put off treatment until the next rest stop or the top of the hill, you may end up dealing with a full-blown blister.

CONSUMER TIP   Follow the boot manufacturer's instructions on waterproofing and care from the outset. Rub talcum powder on your feet to absorb moisture, and remove your innersoles each night to dry them out.

Finding Your Way

With your head and feet outfitted correctly, you're almost ready to start planning that first trip. First you need to be familiar with two basics.

Maps

A map is invaluable in planning a hike. And even on well-marked trails, a map keeps you on track when you run into the unexpected. It's beyond the scope of this book to teach detailed map and compass skills, but a few rudiments can get you started learning—and experience and practice in the field are the true path to proficiency. Don't think you have to be an expert map reader your first times out—especially if you hike with more experienced people. You can learn as your other skills and experience develop.

To become proficient, take along a map of the hike even if hiking with a group. Take advantage of the learning opportunity to look at the map often and figure out your position. Track your progress as if you were by yourself. And be quick to ask your more experienced companions, "How do you know that?" if you don't see the cues they pick up on.

Checking a map in Rocky Mountain National Park, Colorado.

SAFETY TIP Get in the habit of looking for landmarks—an odd-shaped peak, a rock formation, the direction a stream is running. Pay attention to the position of the sun and the direction the wind is blowing. Such cues can keep you oriented.

Guidebooks often contain maps of the hikes they describe. For dayhikes in particular, the guidebook map is often all you'll need.

Topographical maps (also called topo maps, contour maps, quadrangles, and quads) are the best kind for hiking. Hikers love them because they show the lay of the land in detail. Mountains, valleys, and canyons are all visible as contour lines, almost like a 3-D map. By counting the contour lines you can tell how much a trail climbs or descends, a good indicator of the hike's difficulty. (Check the key to see how many feet or meters of change each line represents.)

These maps also show streams, springs, and other water sources, an important feature when planning a backpacking trip. (Also consult a guidebook to make sure the stream you're counting on isn't dry part of the year.)

Topo maps are available for most hiking destinations in the western world. They are the accepted standard, even though most U.S. Geological Survey (USGS) maps, at least, are out of date. They show trails that no longer exist, but do not show trails and roads that have been constructed since the map was last updated—which can be 20 or more years ago.

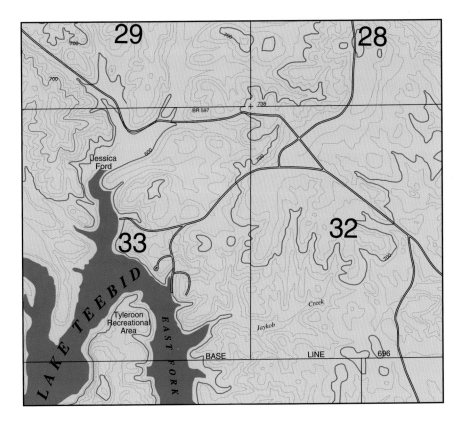

Often you can overcome topo maps' shortcomings by using them in combination with a map from a national park, national forest, or other public land management agency. These agency maps usually show the trails, roads, campgrounds, developments, boundaries, and features such as streams but do not have contour lines.

Most national park maps reliably show existing trails. But they are very large scale and not designed for navigation. U.S. Forest Service maps are

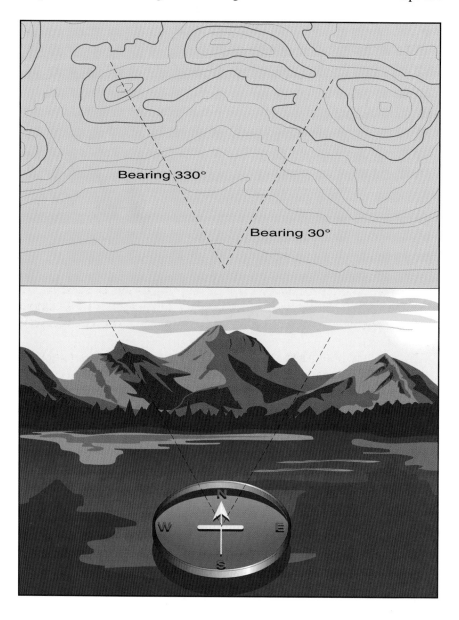

generally of a more useful scale and show more features, but they often show trails that are no longer maintained well enough to be followed. You need to obtain reliable advice before setting out.

Some of the best maps are published by trail clubs and commercial publishers like Trails Illustrated. Some are printed on waterproof, tear-resistant plastic material, great for use in the field. The best are based on the USGS maps, updated and adapted to show areas of interest to hikers. Before printing a new edition the publishers confirm what changes have occurred and which trails actually exist.

Even these maps are not always the perfect solution. For example, maps that cover an entire national park can be so large in scale that you can't interpret the features as you can on the USGS quads. Often, the best solution is to use them with USGS quads.

SAFETY TIP   Keep your map handy. Many hikers have made wrong turns when they couldn't be bothered to pull a map out of their packs. Fold the map to show the area you need to read and protect it from rain in a sealable plastic bag.

Compass

The map's steadfast companion is the compass. Its use is based on the principle that its magnetized needle points generally north. A simple compass, one without sighting mirrors and the like, is sufficient for trail needs.

The needle pivots within a fluid-filled compartment. Surrounding the compartment is a dial marking off 360 degrees—each degree defining a certain direction. Zero (and 360) degrees are north, 90 degrees is east, 180 degrees is south, and 270 degrees is west. (And 135 degrees is southeast and so on.)

The needle does not point to the north pole (called true north or geographic north), but to "magnetic north," a point in northern Canada. The difference between where the needle points and true north is known as the *declination*, and the declination varies according to where you are. In the eastern United States, eastern Canada, and western Europe, compasses point to the west of true north; in the western United States, western Canada, and eastern Europe, compasses point to the east of true north.

USGS quads show schematically the declination for the area they cover. You move the dial according to the declination so it aligns with true north—which is the north shown on your map.

You can practice your map and compass skills at home by obtaining a topographic map of your area. (Your local outdoors store should have them, or you can order from the sources listed in the appendix.)

Work with the map by itself first. If you're like most hikers, on the trail you'll use maps much more than your compass.

PRACTICE MAP AND COMPASS SKILLS

Map

1. Go to a viewpoint where you can see distinctive features of the landscape.
2. Orient the map so it aligns with these features as you see them; that is, hold it so that when you sight along the map, a nearby hill lines up with its position on the map, or so a stream or bridge is in the position shown.
3. Spend time studying the map. Pick a feature represented on the map and see if you can find that point on the ground. Soon you'll start to see how contour lines that form a bull's-eye on the map correspond to a hilltop, how lines too close together to read are a cliff, how a collection of concentric Vs can be either a spur ridge or, if a blue line runs through them, a stream valley.

Compass

1. Lay down your compass on the map and align it to true north according to the declination.
2. Align your map to true north, using your compass.
3. If the landmarks line up as well as they did when you lined them up by sight in the exercise we just described, you did it correctly. If not, try again.
4. For a more complicated exercise, pick two landmarks you can recognize and that are marked clearly on the map.
5. Take a "bearing" on them: Raise the compass to your eye level. Keep the compass oriented so the needle is pointing to north on your dial, but hold it so you can look across the dial directly at the landmark. Note the number on the dial's circle of degrees that lies along this sighting line. This is the bearing to that landmark from your location.
6. Draw a line on your map, starting from the landmark and running in your direction, that corresponds to the direction of this bearing.
7. Take a bearing on a second landmark and draw a similar line.
8. If you've done everything right, the point where these two lines intersect is your location.

Knowing how to take a bearing can help you in important ways. If you don't know where you are but can recognize landmarks, you can figure out your location. If you know where you are, you can identify a landmark by taking a bearing on it and checking the name on your map. (Sometimes these can be done by good map readers with the map only.) If you've lost the trail and must travel cross-country, you can take a bearing that will lead you to a road or trail.

A compass also can help you choose which trail to take at a junction in a thick forest.

An amazing new navigational aid is becoming so light and inexpensive that it may soon become practical for the hiker. A global positioning system receiver can use satellite data to give you an accurate fix on your latitude, longitude, and altitude anywhere in the world. The receiver's cost of several hundred dollars, however, has a long way to drop before it becomes competitive with the simple compass.

Planning a Trip

Assuming you know where you want to hike (see chapter 5 if you need suggestions), look for a hiking guide to that area in your local library, outdoors store, bookstore, or trail club. You'll find guides to most of the best places to hike, including national parks; statewide guidebooks that identify hidden treasures; and formats such as *50 Hikes in the Home Range*. A good guidebook provides a wealth of information on the length and difficulty of particular trails, where to find water, suggested hikes, weather, seasonal conditions, special considerations, and more.

Write for maps of the area from the land managers, hiking club, or map agency. If you plan to camp, ask about requirements, regulations, and permits. Rules vary widely, and will sometimes affect your campsite possibilities and, thus, choice of hikes. Some jurisdictions limit how many people are allowed in certain areas; others have designated huts or camping spots that you must reserve in advance.

Study the maps and guidebooks and think about your goals. If you want to climb a peak or hike to a certain waterfall, you'll probably hike in and out on the same trail. But for the most variety of experience, look for circular routes—called circuit hikes—that return you to the start without retracing your steps. Or you can hike from trailhead A to trailhead B by taking two cars and working a shuttle, leaving a car at the end, then driving in the other car to the start.

For planning your hikes, the next obvious question is, How far can you go? Individuals vary so greatly that your experience will answer this question much better than any guidelines we might give.

© Blaine Harrington III

Maps and books will guide you anywhere—such as to the shadow of Mt. Blanc in the French Alps.

Hikers never think just in terms of distance, but always in terms of distance plus elevation gain. You walk uphill much more slowly than you walk on the flat and it's much more tiring. A trail that gains 500 feet per mile (152 m per 1.6 km) is a steady climb. A trail that gains 1,000 feet per mile (305 m per 1.6 km) is extremely steep. Steep descents may slow you down but rarely as much as a steep ascent.

Another important consideration is the trail surface. You can't walk as fast on narrow and rocky trails, where you have to think about where to put each foot, as you can on abandoned dirt roads that have been turned into trails, where striding is easy and rhythmic.

CALCULATE HIKING TIMES

1. For hiking without an overnight pack, a common rule used in guidebooks is to allow a half hour for each mile (1.6 km) plus a half hour for each 1,000 feet (305 m) of elevation gain. So, for a 3-mile (4.8-km) hike with a 1,000-foot (305-m) elevation gain you should allow two hours. This refers to actual walking time and does not include stops for snacking or gazing.
2. A beginning backpacker should allow 40 minutes to an hour per mile (1.6 km), with an extra hour for each 1,000 feet (305 m) of elevation gain.

Walking with a pack on for 7 or 8 hours will tire out most people. So plan to cover 5 to 10 miles (8 to 16 km) a day with the upper figure applying only to very easy terrain.

Allow yourself time to get into camp early with energy left to take a dip in the creek, check out the view from a nearby rock, take some photos, set up your tent, and eat a leisurely dinner. Having extra time at your campsite is much better than pushing all day, then stumbling into a campsite exhausted, maybe by flashlight. Remember that sitting on a rock is at least as important a goal as marching across the map. Keep in mind the season and how many hours of daylight you'll have. Give yourself a comfortable cushion of time before sunset, and remember that the sun disappears much sooner if there's a mountain it will sink behind.

Of course, your pace may pick up considerably after you've gotten a lot of trail distance under your feet. Many experienced hikers cover 3 miles (4.8 km) per hour, and 2 to 3 miles (3.2 to 4.8 km) per hour with a backpack on. But even trail-hardened backpackers on the Pacific Crest Trail consider 15 or 16 miles (24 or 25.6 km) a productive day. And many people see no reason to ever speed up at all.

Plan your trip in daylong segments, with each day ending at a feasible campsite. Sometimes suitable sites are far apart. (More on how to select campsites later.)

And how long a trip? A week's worth of food is about all most people can carry comfortably.

Allow extra time for the elevation gain on hikes to viewpoints like this one in Yoho National Park in the Canadian Rockies.

Going With Children

Introduce your children to hiking and make it exciting. Provide fun along the way—rocks to scramble on, streams to throw rocks in, candy-laced trail mix to snack on—and get them hooked at an early age. Keep them warm and dry, escalate the adventure component as their strength increases, and you'll be setting the stage for a lifelong family activity that builds strong bonds and fond memories.

Hiking Through the Ages

Before a child is old enough to walk, you can stuff him or her into a kiddie-carrier and take to the trail in your usual fashion, provided someone's willing to come along to carry your gear for you. Remember, you can't judge your baby's clothing needs by the way you feel. You might be peeling off the layers, sweating from exertion, while your baby sits motionless in the pack, growing chillier.

When your youngster becomes a toddler, hiking takes on a very different flavor, alien to most adults but with its own rewards. Anyone who's ever taken a walk with a 2-year-old knows the creeping pace, the intense examination of every new shape and texture. So take advantage of this period in your child's life: Bring along a macro lens camera and a magnifying glass and enjoy a close scrutiny of a short stretch of trailside with your child.

Even at this stage, give your child a little pack with no more weight than a windbreaker and a stuffed animal friend. Your child will see you with your pack and feel more grown up and capable if wearing one too. Make sure your child has good outdoors clothing—small boots and synthetic layers are available. It's not "wasted" money because just as the garments you buy for the trail keep you warm and dry at football games, your child's hiking clothing will double as outside playwear at home.

This suggestion won't win the dental seal of approval, but candy works well as a desperation incentive with children past the toddler stage but still prone to dawdling, boredom, and the "carry me" syndrome. Small rewards, such as one M&M for every additional 5 minutes a boy or girl hikes onward, help the whole family reach the destination.

By age 6, most youngsters can hike their years in miles and often surprise you with their ability to hike far and high. One 6-year-old, who had to be coaxed along via the "Hershey carrot" method the summer before, climbed 4,000 feet (1,219 m) on an 11-mile (17.6-km) trip on Wyoming's fabled Grand Teton Mountain. Another 6-year-old hiked the Appalachian Trail from Georgia to Maine in one summer.

Once youngsters hit those middle elementary school years, they're in their element, racing up the trail, anxious to see what's around the next bend. But they can't carry much weight until their teenage years, so if you want to trek deep into the backcountry, look for an outfitter that organizes family trips with pack animals to carry all the food, pots, clothing, tents, and sleeping bags.

Hiking and backpacking are ideal family activities where you can share real adventure outside the constricting confines of your car. And if you hook children on the outdoors early, they may even want to take vacations with you when they're teenagers!

© Kent & Donna Dannen

It's never too early to introduce your child to the outdoors.

Tips for Hiking With Kids

Hiking and backpacking with kids can be a lot of fun but you must keep safety in mind.

- Dress your children in easy-to-spot-in-the-woods neon colors and give them whistles they can blow if they get separated from you.
- Water is heavy. Plan trips with reliable water sources along the route and bring iodine tablets and lemon flavoring.

- Avoid using bug repellent containing high concentrations of DEET on children's skin. Under age 2: no more than one application in 24 hours. Under age 6: no repeated applications of a concentration greater than 15%.
- Avoid high elevations during the early years. The younger the child, the greater the risk of altitude sickness.
- Make sure your youngster has good sunglasses when you're ready to head for high peaks and snowfields.

Eating on the Trail

The best foods to eat for energy are complex carbohydrates, but they just don't stick to your ribs. So snacks are as important as meals in both dayhiking and backpacking. Many hikers and backpackers never stop for an identifiable lunch—instead they take frequent munch breaks.

When you begin to tire, a drink of water and a few mouthfuls of food can revive you to a surprising extent. That out-of-gas feeling often comes from depleted fuel stores instead of muscular exhaustion. Keep some snacks, such as a bag of trail mix or dried fruit, in a handy side pocket for a quick energy boost.

Backpacking Food

Backpacking's weight limitations restrict the variety of food people carry, but this restriction is offset by one of the principles of being outdoors—food tastes so much better there. Any food. In fact, we never met a trail meal we didn't like! Countless times after a long day's hike, we've raved about that night's very ordinary combination of pasta, cheese, and spices, saying, "We should try this at home" and knowing full well that the irreplaceable magical ingredients were the fresh air and exercise.

Most of a food's weight is in the water it contains. But because water is available on almost any hike you'll do, you can add it to dried foods at your campsite.

You can simplify menu planning by buying light, convenient, freeze-dried foods at an outdoors specialty store. Instead of figuring out ingredients and shopping for them, you can pick up a variety of these already-put-together meals. Most are packaged in foil pouches. Just pour in boiling water and wait a few minutes while the liquid soaks into the food. You can eat right out of the pouch, leaving no dirty dishes. Because you're only heating water instead of cooking, you use a minimum of fuel.

Freeze-dried food is expensive, however, even more expensive than it first appears because you can't believe the cheery labels that say "serves two." "Serves one" is more accurate, and then only if you have additional items on your dinner menu. After a hard day on the trail, it's easy to polish off a "dinner-for-four" yourself!

Food from the supermarket takes a little more preparation and planning but is a lot less expensive and not necessarily heavier. For a cold cereal breakfast, mix dried milk and water and pour it over granola or muesli. (Avoid flake cereals, which will get crushed in your pack.) For warmth, add hot water to instant oatmeal or cream of wheat in single-serving sizes with flavorings added. Our favorite is 1-minute oatmeal cooked with dried fruit bits and raisins, which become plump and juicy.

Most backpackers don't stop to cook a lunch, but munch away on items like the ones listed on pages 58-59.

It's best to plan easy-to-cook, one-pot dinners for several reasons: You'll probably be carrying a one-burner stove; you'll use less fuel; cleanup is easier; and the fewer the pots, the lighter the load.

CONSUMER TIP   Shop according to where you're going. On trips where you have to carry all your water—the beach, the desert, or a dry mountain ridge—a can of ready-to-eat food ends up weighing less than noodles that require you to drain off a lot of cooking water.

There are many noodle-based or rice-based mixes available (Lipton makes a good variety). Or start with a starch—rice, instant potatoes, or noodles—and add dried milk, a dab of margarine, maybe some freeze-dried vegetables and, if you want more protein, a small can of meat or extra dried cheese. (The milk and margarine add both flavor and calories. Margarine will keep in a plastic container for several days in all but the hottest conditions.) Then mix in herbs, flavor packets, soup mixes, dried onions, garlic powder, Tabasco—let your imagination take over.

COOKING TIP   Many stoves seem to have little heat control between "off" and "blow torch." Add extra water to foods that need to simmer, and stir often. Also consider that at higher elevations water boils at a lower temperature, so food takes longer to cook.

Eating Out

Day Trips

On a dayhike, you can carry whatever you're willing to cart along—sandwiches, cheese and crackers, leftover pizza, fruit, granola and energy bars, cookies, cans of pudding, candy. It's better to maintain a regular flow of energy by snacking often on dried fruit and trail mix (nuts, raisins, etc.) than to gorge on a three-sandwich lunch.

Weekend Overnights

For a weekend night or two, your choices are wide open. In warm weather, you could dispense with a stove and carry only sandwiches, cereal, hard-boiled eggs, and other foods that require no cooking. You could opt for luxury over lightness, carrying in frozen meat (weather permitting) that defrosts in your pack and hardy vegetables such as potatoes, cucumbers, and broccoli.

Or carry the myriad foods available in cans: Chinese dinners, stew, chili, tamales, lobster bisque. Or stick with light backpacking foods.

Weeklong Treks

On trips of more than a couple days, weight is a primary concern. The easiest choice is freeze-dried backpacking food, but you also can shop at the supermarket.

Breakfast: Hot or cold cereal, "instant breakfast," breakfast bars, dried eggs.

Lunch and snacks: crackers and cheese; sandwiches of peanut butter with jam or honey, hard salami, sardines, canned fish or meat on crush-resistant breads like pita; food bars; dried fruit; trail mix; nuts; chocolate; cookies; granola bars.

Dinner: freeze-dried meals in pouches; macaroni and cheese; packaged noodle or rice dinners, perhaps with cans of meat and freeze-dried vegetables.

Dessert: instant pudding; dried fruit soaked, sweetened, and cooked; candy bars; freeze-dried ice cream.

Accompaniments such as dried soup, instant coffee, tea, cocoa, and bouillon weigh little and add much to enjoyment.

Fluids

The other key to keeping your muscles well supplied is to take in plenty of fluids. Drink often, before you're thirsty. On a dayhike, carry any fluids you want (water, juice, sport drinks). When backpacking, you'll need to find water along the way and usually treat it. Many people carry powdered drink mixes—fruit flavors, protein enhancers, electrolyte replacements. Flavorings encourage you to drink because they taste good, mask the taste of iodine pills, and boost your energy. Water is heavy—about 2 pounds a quart (1 kg per liter)—but don't skimp to try to lighten your load. You'll risk greater discomfort if you run out before getting to the next source.

You can even create a homemade version of a freeze-dried meal pouch using foods such as couscous and instant rice that are prepared by simply adding boiling water. Pour meal-size portions along with herbs and other accompaniments in sealable plastic freezer bags at home, then just add water at your campsite. (Most plastic bags are not rated to work at these temperatures but still do—test this out at home before you go.) It's bound to be a great meal if you've hiked all day and you eat it outdoors!

CONSUMER TIP   For gourmet meal ideas, check backpacking cookbooks, which are usually on the shelves in outdoors stores next to the guidebooks. Backpackers have come up with amazingly tasty recipes.

How Much Food Is Enough?

Your caloric demands depend on your weight, age, gender, level of activity, and metabolism. But out on the trail it seems as if you always want and need twice as much as at home—especially if you have a sedentary desk job. Just walking rapidly burns 300 calories per hour, and you burn a lot more if you're going up steep grades carrying a loaded pack. Hiking 7 hours or more on a challenging trail, your energy requirements could easily rise to 4,000 calories and even top 5,000 calories a day, double your at-home consumption.

That's why you'll see backpackers squinting at the "Nutrition Information" on food labels, checking to see which packages contain the most calories per serving (just the opposite of dieters!). When you do this you'll soon notice that proteins and complex carbohydrates like oatmeal and rice provide about 100 calories per dried ounce (28 g). Fat contains a little more than twice the calories per ounce that proteins and carbos do.

With a good balance between carbohydrates, protein, and fat, you can get those 4,000-plus calories a day in about 2 to 2-1/4 pounds (0.9 to 1 kg).

Plan each meal of the trip and add extra emergency supplies. You could be delayed by all sorts of things: an injury, a storm, getting lost, miscalculating the distance, or even dawdling too much because a trail is too beautiful. An extra day's rations is a good idea.

You should also pack extra hot drinks that can quickly warm a chilled hiker.

DIET BALANCING

Although most health-conscious people are trying to limit the fat in their diets, it definitely has value on the trail. Its high calories-to-the-ounce ratio allows you to cut down the weight of the food component of your load. But more important, it metabolizes more slowly, so it provides energy long after the carbohydrates have been burned off.

Cold weather increases caloric demands, so winter hikers often add even more fat to their trip diets. The "fat calories" help sustain their body temperature during a long cold night. What a good excuse to take along those chocolate bars!

Protein, like fat, burns more slowly than carbohydrates in the muscular oven. Most backpackers get their protein from cheese, freeze-dried dinners with meat, beef jerky, hard salami, "meal bars," nuts, peanut butter, and cans of meat or fish. Cheese keeps satisfactorily, except in the hottest conditions.

One disadvantage of fats and proteins is that they require more oxygen to burn than carbohydrates do. This could make a big difference at high altitudes when your leg muscles are screaming for oxygen.

Can I Carry All That?

Your equipment and food pile may now look impossibly large, making you wonder if you can get it all on your back.

The standard guideline is that the average man can carry about a third of his body weight and the average woman can carry a fourth of her body weight (and, with training, match the male standard of one-third). So a 130-pound (59-kg) woman can carry about 32 pounds (14.4 kg), and a 210-pound (95-kg) man can carry about 70 pounds (31.5 kg).

But there's a big difference between what you *can* carry and what you *want* to carry. These weight levels are really out of your comfort zone. You'll enjoy the trip more and be able to go farther if you carry less. To be comfortable, aim for a fifth of your body weight.

And these percentages assume you are not overweight. Body weight in the form of fat counts against your ability to carry more on your back.

Such rules of thumb help if you want to weigh your pack to see if it's reasonable, but here's another way to look at it: If a day's supply of food weighs a little more than 2 pounds (0.9 kg), a week's supply is 15 pounds (6.75 kg). Added to the necessary accoutrements in your pack, that makes for a pretty full load. Most people don't go for much more than a week without resupplying.

Packing Your Pack

Before starting to load your pack, get everything pack-ready. This final preparation can be surprisingly time consuming, so allow plenty of time and don't rush it.

PACK YOUR GEAR

Get Gear Ready

1. Repackage your food as necessary. Take no jars—they're not only heavy but also dangerous if broken. Jams, peanut butter, and margarine can be put in refillable, squeezable plastic tubes, which are available in outdoors equipment stores. Transfer food from store packages that can leak to sturdy, sealable plastic bags. Be sure to include the cooking directions. (Some people organize food in separate stuff sacks or plastic bags by meals—all the dinners together—or by the day.)

2. Pack the tent stakes in a separate bag so they can't puncture the tent.

3. Put your clothes in plastic bags or stuff sacks as extra waterproofing, and line the sleeping bag's stuff sack with a plastic bag.

4. To make everything fit more easily, look for ways to reduce the bulk, such as filling the cookpot with food.

When everything is ready to go, put it all in one spot, and get out your checklist. Check each item off as you load your pack.

Load Your Pack

1. Keep items you'll need during the day handy. Maps, lunch, snacks, water bottle, pullover or windbreaker for rest stops, moleskin, and first aid kit, for example, should be on top or in outside pockets.

2. Avoid contaminating food and cookware; pack your fuel bottle and stove in a separated area, such as a side pocket.

3. Be careful that sharp-edged items don't poke holes in the pack or in other gear.

4. Load the sides evenly so you don't list to port or starboard when you walk.

Your other main concern in pack loading is how to distribute the weight. You'll load the pack differently depending on whether it's an external frame or an internal frame, and depending on whether you're a man or a woman. We find an external-frame pack easier to load than an internal frame

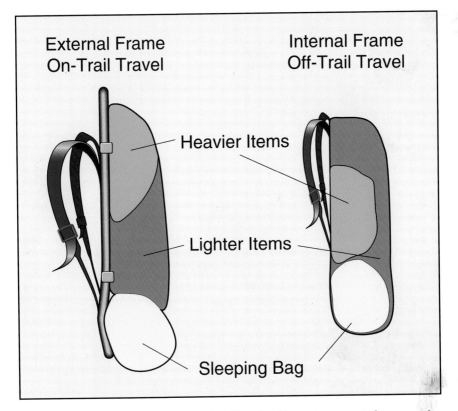

External Frame
On-Trail Travel

Internal Frame
Off-Trail Travel

Heavier Items

Lighter Items

Sleeping Bag

because it stands up on its own, holding itself out to accept the gear. An internal frame depends on the equipment in it to hold its shape. Sometimes if you remove an item, your whole structure collapses; keep that in mind while packing.

If you're a man, load an external-frame pack with the heavy gear on top, about as high as possible and close to your back. This brings the load up over your hips and feet, making it easier to carry.

This packing order means that sleeping bags go on the bottom—lashed to the frame below the pack. Lighter gear (such as clothing) goes in the bottom of the packbag, with heavier things (food) above it. The tent, usually the heaviest piece of gear, can be lashed to the bar atop an external frame. The upper pockets can hold the relatively heavy water bottles, fuel, and lunch.

If you're a woman, you'll probably find your load more comfortable if you pack slightly differently. Since your relatively shorter torso and longer legs give you a center of gravity around the hips, it's usually better not to put the heavy items as high as for men, whose center of gravity is around the diaphragm. Start by following the same general pattern as described for men, but experiment until the center of gravity is right for you. Some women are more comfortable with the heaviest gear on the bottom and lightest gear on top.

With an internal frame, the sleeping bag always goes in the bottom, giving the pack definition. Then the rest of the loading depends on the kind of hiking you'll be doing. For most trail walking you'll want a packing order similar to that for external-frame packs. For rougher terrain, rock scrambling, or other activities where balance is important, keep the heavy gear lower and closer to the body. Women may find this latter approach more comfortable in all terrain and thus should experiment. Because there is no frame between you and your gear, put a soft layer (such as a sleeping pad) closest to your body.

The final trick to pack loading is developing a system so you know where everything is. At one time or another, you'll want every item in a hurry. You don't want to be searching for insect repellent while the mosquitoes feast on your neck, wondering where your flashlight is in the dark, or pulling gear out in the rain while you search for your poncho. The surprisingly large number of individual items in your pack are easier to find if you put like items together—such as the kitchen equipment, repair kit, or small, easy-to-lose widgets.

Consider organizing gear in color-coded stuff sacks—one for dinner food, one for breakfast food, one for clothes, etc. Label outside pockets with pieces of tape—one might be the stove pouch, another the water bottle pouch. Develop a little compulsiveness and foolish consistency. Decide that the first aid kit always goes in the top pouch and the flashlight always goes in the bottom pouch, and that's where they'll be when you need to find them.

SAFETY TIP   Set up your tent at home before going on a trip so you're familiar with its workings. Don't be left standing in the rain trying to read the instructions. And learn about your stove before you set off by actually cooking on it.

PUT YOUR PACK ON

The easiest way to put your pack on is to place it on a raised rock, log, or anything that allows you to slip your arms into the shoulder straps, then stand up. Better yet, get your hiking companion to pick it up from behind you so you can slip into it like putting on a jacket. Lacking a platform or a willing partner, follow these steps:

1. Grasp the shoulder straps.
2. Swing the pack up on your hip or thigh.
3. Slip the arm on that side into the strap.
4. Swing the pack around behind you and slip the other arm in.
5. Properly done, the momentum of the pack never quite stops.

Picking a Campsite

You've loaded your pack and hiked into the woods. Now where do you set up camp? First, you need to comply with local restrictions, such as no camping above a certain elevation or in certain areas. Second, you need a tent site reasonably free of the rocks and roots that can make you wake up reaching for an aspirin and level enough that you don't roll off your sleeping pad.

The site should be somewhat sheltered from wind and precipitation and near a water source so you don't have to carry all your water in with you. If you pick a stream valley or a lake as your destination, you'll probably find a spot with all these attributes. (But remember to set up at least 50 feet (15 m) from the water. If you can't find a spot wide enough for your tent that

At day's end a scenic tent site makes for a contented backpacker.

is far enough from the water, you should walk farther away to do your cooking and washing.)

As you gain experience, you'll develop your own likes and dislikes—a good rock to sit on while you cook, a good view from the tent. You won't always find the ideal site. And when you don't, you must adjust to it instead of trying to make it adjust to you. It's fine to move small rocks and downed branches, but never cut vegetation to make space for your tent or for bedding. Don't dig a moat around your tent.

Check the slope of the site before setting up your tent by lying down to see how it feels. You'll probably sleep better with your head higher than your feet rather than vice versa. Is anything poking you in the back? We like tent sites under conifer trees, which tend to have soft duff and less vegetation under them.

In most places, good campsites are uncommon enough that they are used over and over. Studies show that efforts to let overused spots recover are not having the desired effects—the overused sites are not coming back even after years of being closed.

A researcher who has studied the problem recommends that if you are in a heavily used area, use a heavily used site. In little-visited areas, choose spots that have never been used and leave no trace that you were there.

When You Get Home

When you return from backpacking, instead of shoving your gear into a closet, take a few steps to increase its longevity. Air dry the tent and sleeping bag thoroughly. Don't store the sleeping bag in its stuff sack (this shortens the life of its lofting ability). Store it in a larger sack or garbage bag. Wash your cook kit well. Hold your pack upside down and shake out debris. Now put your gear away, organized so that when an irresistible day for a campout comes, you can be packed in time to enjoy the sunset from your favorite ridge.

4

HIKING AND BACKPACKING SAFELY

Once again, Hulda Crooks hit the trail near Lone Pine, California, and climbed 11 miles (17.6 km) to the top of 4,495-foot (4,418-m) Mt. Whitney, highest mountain in the "lower 48." She liked that trip so much, she made it 23 times between the ages of 66 and 93.

At 67, "Grandma" Gatewood became the first woman to solo hike the 2,100-mile (3,380-km) Appalachian Trail. She enjoyed it so much, she did it two more times.

If Hulda Crooks and Grandma Gatewood could hike, certainly you can. The questions are, How much can you do, and how do you match your fitness level to the trails on a map?

Is Your Body Ready?

If you can walk on the street, you can walk on at least some trails right now. But how far? You probably can walk as many hours on the trail as you can on the street. But you won't cover as much ground because trail walking is more difficult. The typical street pace is about 3 miles (4.8 km) per hour. On trails, it's more often 2 miles (3.2 km) per hour (and with a full pack, 1 mile [1.6 km] per hour).

Using that very rough rule, you can travel about two thirds as far carrying a daypack on a trail as walking on the street and about one third as far carrying a full pack. So when you start backpacking, you'll cover only about half the distance you did on your dayhikes. This guideline does not take into account the difficulty of the trail, your hiking style, and other factors. As mentioned in the previous chapter, you should increase your estimate of hiking time to include elevation gain. How much the elevation gain will slow you down is related to your conditioning level—we've seen really fit people climbing as if the hills were level.

© Larry Dunmire/Photo Network

Improving your fitness will help you reach those special places far from the road.

Improving Your Fitness

If you're worried about not being fit enough to hike or you want to enhance the experience, an exercise program will help. There are several reasons to get in better shape before hitting the trail.

The first is to increase the distance you can travel comfortably. The best attractions tend to be a little farther from the road.

Second, you'll increase your enjoyment (and, to be honest, decrease your pain). When you get tired, you tend to bow your head and watch your feet, wishing for the end of the trail instead of being alert to its beauties and nuances. Exercises can build your strength, decrease your potential for injuries, and help problem areas such as weak knees.

When you go backpacking, you won't find it easy to suddenly gain the weight of a heavy pack and then walk up and down mountains. The better condition you're in before heading out, the easier your adjustment because your load will feel lighter. If you have only a couple of weeks for vacation, much better to enjoy each day than to spend some of them getting broken in on the trail.

The most important factor for hiking enjoyment is cardiovascular fitness; next is muscular strength. Most exercises to improve cardiovascular fitness also work your hiking muscles.

Obviously, the main muscles used in hiking are in the legs, although abdominal and other upper-body strength helps, especially for backpacking. A strong heart gets you up a hill, but strong legs get you down. With each step downhill, gravity pulls your body forward. Your legs, particularly your knees, absorb shock at each step and at the same time have to restrain you from pitching farther forward.

As always, before greatly increasing your activity level, consult your physician.

Specificity of Training

The best way to get in shape for any sport is through "specificity of training," trainer jargon that means to train for an activity, do that activity. To get in shape for hiking, go hiking. To train for backpacking, go backpacking.

But how do you go hiking if you don't live next door to a national park? Simply look for opportunities to walk. Walk places you usually drive. Go for a walk before work, at lunch, after work. Instead of taking the elevator, take the stairs.

Find parks near your home and go for brisk walks as often as possible, for a half hour, an hour, or whatever you can. Include some hills and gradually increase your time and distance. If you can't get to hills, hike up and down stairwells—a great office building workout on your lunch hour and even on business trips!

Brisk walks in your local park will help you get in shape for wilderness trails.

Then carry your daypack, loaded with those items "you shouldn't leave home without" plus your water bottles. This will show you how this extra weight affects your pace and endurance.

When you begin thinking about a backpacking expedition, start carrying a pack (containing equipment and food) and see how far you can hike around home. And don't avoid those hills! You'll build strength and condition the stress points where your body will bear weight—hips, shoulders, and collarbone area.

Cardiovascular Training

Current conventional wisdom is that three aerobic workouts a week will improve or maintain cardiovascular fitness. An aerobic workout simply means one that makes your heart and lungs work hard at what's called target pulse rate.

Your target pulse rate is 60% to 90% of your maximum heart rate, which is your age subtracted from 220. Or use a less formal gauge: If you're breathing heavily and still can converse with a partner, you're at the right level. If you can sing, you're not working hard enough. If you're gasping and can barely talk, you're working too hard.

The workout need last only about 20 minutes at your target rate, with 5 minutes of reduced activity to warm up and 5 minutes to cool down.

You can get this workout from jogging, bicycling (especially uphill), running stairs, stair-climbing machines, rowing machines, Nordic skiing machines, and the like. But you also can get it walking briskly up a steep hill, which subjects your knees to less stress than, for instance, jogging does. A loaded pack increases the intensity.

Muscle-Strengthening Exercises

For additional strengthening, if you have access to free weights or weight machines, work your quadriceps, hamstrings, and calves, but also do some upper-body pumping and pushing. You'll get the best results from machines and weights, but you can try the following exercises at home. The first two strengthen the quadriceps muscle at the front of the thigh, the third strengthens the hamstrings at the back of the thigh, and the fourth strengthens the calf muscles.

SEATED LEG LIFTS   Sit on a chair with your feet on the floor. Place a coffee can or towel roll under your knee. Slowly raise the lower portion of your leg, hold for six counts, slowly lower, and relax. Do three sets of 10 repetitions. Add an ankle weight as soon as you can do three sets easily. Start out with 2-pound (0.9-kg) to 3-pound (1.35-kg) weights and gradually add more.

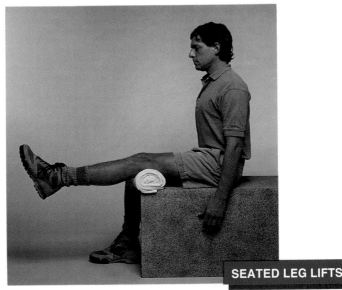

SEATED LEG LIFTS

THE SKIER

Stand with your back against a wall. Lower yourself as if sitting in an imaginary chair and hold this position as long as you can—which won't be long until you build up good thigh strength!

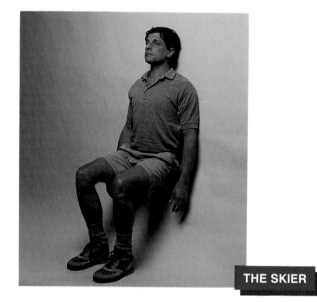

THE SKIER

PRONE LEG LIFTS

Lie on your stomach. Slowly raise your foot until your lower leg is at a 45-degree angle. Hold for six counts, slowly lower, and relax. Repeat 10 times for three sets. Add ankle weights as with seated leg lifts.

PRONE LEG LIFTS

CALF RAISES Stand with your heels hanging off a step or fat telephone book. Rise to your tiptoes, then back again. Repeat 8 to 12 times.

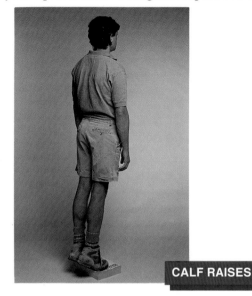

CALF RAISES

For the upper body, do the old standbys like pull-ups and push-ups. Also pay attention to your back and abdomen—strong abdominals can do much to keep your lower back in shape.

ABDOMINAL CRUNCH Lie on your back, feet off the floor, thighs perpendicular to the ground, knees bent at 90 degrees, hands behind head. Curl your upper torso toward the knees, keeping your lower back on the ground. Raise and lower slowly. (You also can do this with your feet on the floor and knees raised.) Avoid raising the small of your back off the ground because it puts undue stress on your back, the problem with the traditional sit-up.

ABDOMINAL CRUNCH

PRONE HYPEREXTENSION   Lie face down with your arms at your sides. Slowly raise your head, upper body, arms, and legs off the floor. Lower them to original position.

PRONE HYPEREXTENSION

Stretching

Stretching is an important part of staying fit, especially when you're building your muscles. A muscle becomes stronger after every workout, but in the process it shortens (which is felt as a tightening). Stretching the muscle counteracts this tightening, which in turn decreases the danger of suffering a pulled muscle or other injury when exercising.

Before stretching, warm your muscles for a few minutes with some easy jogging in place. Then stretch slowly, feeling the pull in the muscle, and hold for 30 seconds. Never bounce.

On a hike where you travel either uphill or downhill a lot, the same muscles are worked in the same way over and over again. Stretching these muscles helps keep them from cramping or being sore the next day.

We recommend the following stretches, which cover the major leg muscles, because they are simple and easy to do on the trail.

CALF AND ACHILLES TENDON STRETCH   Stand 4 feet (1.2 m) from a wall or tree and place your hands on it. Lean forward by bending your elbows, keeping your back straight and heels on the ground. Hold this position, feeling the stretch in your lower legs.

CALF AND ACHILLES TENDON STRETCH

HAMSTRINGS STRETCH   Lift one leg and place your heel on something about the level of your hip—a desk, rock, hood of a car. Grab the elevated ankle and bend forward as far as possible. (Keep the toe of the other foot pointed in the direction of the stretch.) Switch legs.

HAMSTRINGS STRETCH

QUADRICEPS STRETCH   Stand on one foot, grasp the ankle of the leg to be stretched, and pull the foot up to your buttocks. Switch legs. (This is even more effective lying face down on the ground.)

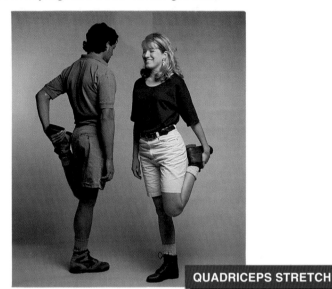

QUADRICEPS STRETCH

Developing Safety Skills

The keys to avoiding injury have more to do with your head than your body. Most threats come from mistakes, misjudgments, and lack of preparation. Knowing what to look out for will enable you to avoid most problems and cope with most mishaps.

 SAFETY TIP   While trails are generally safe, trailhead break-ins have increased in some areas. Don't leave valuables in your car.

Leaving Word

Before heading into the woods, leave your expected route and timetable with someone you trust. Give that person a time you will check in; if you're overdue, that person should alert the police or rangers.

When you finish your hike, be certain to check in so no one goes out looking for you while you're back home having a beer!

Staying Found

The first step in staying found is to keep track of where you are. Even if you're on a clear trail and you think you know where it's going, observe things like landmarks, sun position, and wind direction and stop often to check your map. And stick to trails that are distinct paths, well maintained and well marked, until you've put many miles on your boots.

SAFETY TIP If you step off the trail to relieve yourself, tell someone in your group, or at least leave your pack on the trail. The people coming behind you will know where you are, and you won't be left behind.

Many, but by no means all, of these trails will be marked with "blazes"—in the eastern United States by paint blotches, in the western United States by ax marks on trees. Blazes may be used to color-code trails. For example, the Appalachian Trail is blazed with white rectangles, 2 inches by 6 inches (5 cm by 15 cm). Above tree line and in canyon country, trails are often

Dudley/Seaborg

Orange paint blazes mark the Florida Trail.

marked with rock piles called cairns. Other markings are plastic and metal tags in trees and posts in the ground. When you see a double blaze—two blazes on the same tree—keep your eyes open because a change such as a junction or a major turn in the trail is ahead.

Sometimes blazes are faded or far apart. Sometimes signs are missing. And sometimes it's difficult to see a distinct path because the trail has not been maintained. The ability to follow a trail grows with experience, and you should be alert to the cues—leaves ground by boots, the dip formed by the trail, beaten brush, and the difference in width between a narrow game trail made by deer hooves and one made by humans.

© R. Bossi

Cairns can help you find your way above tree line.

EARTH WATCH When trails go up a steep hill, they often zigzag in sharp turns called switchbacks. Switchbacks give the hiker a manageable grade and prevent erosion. If you shortcut between them, you not only could lose the trail, but you would contribute to a gutter-like channel for rainwater that will erode the hillside. Stick to the trail!

Getting Found

If you suddenly find yourself off the trail, stop and ponder how you got there. If you calmly retrace your steps, you probably will find the trail.

If you can't find the trail, stop and consider your situation. Panic and bad choices are your most dangerous threats at this point. Everyone gets a little lost sooner or later, and those who react calmly have the fewest difficulties.

Was the trail following a stream that is still running near you, so you could follow the stream to find the trail? Is there a road that you could take a compass bearing on and head for? Many eastern U.S. mountain ranges consist of little more than a ridge. Hiking downhill eventually will get you out of the mountains, and if you follow a stream it will lead you out because water never runs uphill. But in larger mountain ranges, following a stream may only get you into a canyon.

If you don't feel confident you can get yourself out, don't do anything to make it harder for someone to find you. Stay put! Don't split up your group and don't start wandering aimlessly through the woods. Unless you have a destination in mind and a plan of how to get there, you're likely to walk in circles and never get out.

Eventually someone will come looking for you—that's why you left word where you were going. Find an opening if you're in deep woods—a meadow, a rocky area—and spread out an orange space blanket or other colorful object to make yourself visible. Blow your whistle. Three short blasts are an international distress call. Light a smoky fire, unless you are in an area of forest fire danger.

If you have to spend the night out, find a sheltered spot—between rocks, in a hollowed spot of ground, by a tree trunk. Wrap yourself in your poncho or space blanket and put on your extra clothes *before* you get cold. Put something between you and the ground, because in most conditions you'll lose more warmth to the ground than to the air. Huddle close with others in your party. In an exposed place, shelter from wind is more important than a fire for warmth.

And, again, don't panic. If you feel the creeping surge of fear, hug each other, hug a tree, sing, tell jokes. Remind yourself and each other that you are going to survive, that it's just a temporary inconvenience. You brought extra water and food for just this reason. And after you eat that emergency food you can live for several days without more.

SAFETY TIP   To keep individuals from getting lost or separated from a group, always have the first person along the trail wait at any junction or turn for the others before continuing on or turning in a new direction.

Crossing a Stream

There are a lot more streams than bridges in the backcountry. You can cross many of them on rocks or logs. Use a hiking staff or a stick for balance.

Always unbuckle your hipbelt and sternum strap before you cross. That way if you fall in, you can slip out of your pack instead of being stuck like a turtle on its shell.

If you have to wade, be careful. Don't wade barefoot. Wear your camp shoes if you want to keep your boots dry. Face upstream. Use a staff or stick as a "third leg" support, and move only one foot or the staff at a time. Use your companions for mutual support.

Fast-moving water has more power than people who have not experienced it can believe. A strong current up to your knees can sweep you downstream. If you're not completely confident of a crossing, don't try it; simply turn back. There are plenty of other trails.

Coping With Critters

Seeing creatures big and small in their natural habitats is one reward of hiking. But from the very large to the most minute, critters can cause trouble if you don't take precautions.

Remember these basic rules for large animals, such as moose and bear: Give them a wide berth. Retreat if necessary. Never get between a mother and her young.

Bears

We were two days into the backcountry of Alaska's Denali National Park when we spotted one of the most awe-inspiring sights for any backpacker— a grizzly bear loping toward us over open ground. We were thunderstruck not only by the majesty of the king of the tundra but also because we realized that if he'd wanted to, that bear could have eaten us!

Grizzly bears are about the only North American animals that can think of a human as filet material, and they're found only in Wyoming, Montana, Idaho, Alaska, and western Canada. If you're headed into these areas, read the guidebooks and talk to the rangers about precautions.

You're more likely to encounter black bears, which are abundant in many North American parks and forests. (They come in other color phases, such as brown and cinnamon, but are black bears just the same.) Bears who live near many popular backpacking destinations have learned that campers carry food and have become ingenious at helping themselves to it. (They will almost never bother a hiker during the day; they commit their thievery in camp at dusk or after dark.)

Keeping the appropriate distance from young Dall sheep in Alaska's Denali National Park.

To avoid being victimized, hang your food. If your campsite has a bear cable or pole, take advantage of it. If not, use a tree branch.

Hang your food well before dusk, both to beat the bear before it starts its rounds and to have plenty of time to find a good branch. Hang all your food and anything scented that a bear might mistake for food (such as toothpaste, deodorant, and other toiletries).

Don't leave dirty dishes around; don't cook, eat, or store food in your tent; and don't keep pots and pans and the like in your tent. Leave the pockets of your pack unzipped so bears and other animals can check that they're empty without having to rip them off or chew a hole in them.

Smaller Animals

By hanging your food you will protect it from smaller critters as well, such as raccoons, skunks, porcupines, and mice. These animals also have learned to associate humans with food and to frequent shelters where people often camp.

And don't get too close to such seemingly harmless animals. They can spread diseases such as rabies and bubonic plague. While the threat is remote, there's no sense in taking chances.

HANG YOUR FOOD

1. Divide your food into two equally weighted stuff sacks (use rocks for ballast if the food is too light).
2. Find a branch 25 feet (7.5 m) off the ground.
3. Tie a rope around a rock so you can throw it, and throw your rope over the branch, at least 10 feet (3 m) out from the trunk.
4. Tie the rope to one stuff sack, leaving a large loop hanging from it. Hoist that sack up to the branch by pulling on the rope.
5. Tie the other stuff sack to the other end of the rope, putting any leftover rope inside the bag so it does not hang down. Push this sack up. The other sack will come down to meet it. Use a stick to finish pushing it up. The sacks should meet at least 12 feet (3.6 m) off the ground.
6. To retrieve your food in the morning, hook the stick through the rope loop on the first sack and pull it down.

Snakes

Nothing gives many people that creepy crawly feeling quite like snakes. The fear is out of proportion to reality—most snakes you'll see are not poisonous and many are quite beautiful.

Even the poisonous ones are at least as afraid of you as you are of them, and they will do all they can to avoid you if you don't surprise them. Don't step or put your hands into places that you can't see. Don't step over a log without looking. Don't put your hand blindly up onto a rock ledge. Don't stumble around camp without a light at night, when snakes are active.

Check your guidebook for specifics on poisonous snakes that might be in the area. Poisonous snakebites occur every year (although very few hikers are bitten). The vast majority of bites are not fatal.

First aid for snakebite has been controversial, with the old "cut-and-suck" method criticized for doing more harm than good. However, at least two books on outdoors medicine written by physicians recommend use of a relatively new product called the Extractor, a suction device that requires no incisions. If used within 3 minutes, 35% of the venom can be removed, according to one doctor. It also can help remove venom from bee stings and insect bites.

While removing some of the venom may help, it is obviously not a cure. The only actual treatment for snakebite is antivenin, which must be administered under medical supervision.

But keep these points in mind. In up to 25% of rattlesnake bites, no venom is injected. The effects of the bite correlate to the victim's body weight. Snakebites are rarely fatal to healthy adults, but a small child would need evacuation by any means possible to obtain treatment within hours.

Biting Insects

Mosquitoes, no-see-ums (midges), blackflies, chiggers, and other insects will be glad to feast on your body, a bite at a time. At certain times of the year, their swarms can drive the strongest people crazy.

You can cope by following these strategies. First, keep clothing and netting between you and your tormentors. Wearing long sleeves and tucking long pants into your socks will help. In extreme cases use a "bug hat" with a mesh veil that covers your face and neck. Your tent may be the only safe place at dusk, when the insects are more active.

Second, avoid places where they congregate. Mosquitoes, for example, need water to breed and are thick in damp and swampy places. Don't set up your tent on an anthill. In the southeastern United States, chiggers crawl aboard when you sit on a log.

Your third line of defense is repellent sprays and liquids. The most effective ones contain a chemical called DEET. Look for it on the label.

Ticks

Most bug bites cause an itch or rash that disappears after a couple of days. Tick bites, however, can be serious because they can spread disease, including Lyme disease and Rocky Mountain spotted fever.

To protect yourself from ticks, use DEET-based insect repellent (or Permanone Tick Repellent, for use on clothing only). Check yourself often, including your hair, and pick ticks off while they're still looking for a soft place to bite. It's easy to spot the dog tick, not so easy to spot the Lyme disease-carrying deer tick, which is about the size of the period at the end of this sentence.

If a tick has started to bite, grasp it close to the mouth parts with tweezers and pull it straight out with steady pressure, taking care not to leave the head in.

Cases of Lyme disease have been reported all over the United States. (A related disorder called Bannworth's syndrome has been reported in Britain, continental Europe, and Australia.) Usually a distinctive red rash in a bull's-eye around the bite appears after 3 days to a month. About the same time, flu-like symptoms appear (muscle aches, fatigue, fever, nausea, etc.). If untreated, the disease can cause serious neurological and arthritic complications.

Rocky Mountain spotted fever, despite its name, is most common in the eastern United States. After a 2- to 14-day incubation, a fever begins abruptly, followed by a red-spotted rash on hands and feet that spreads to the trunk. Untreated, it can be fatal.

Of course, there is much more variation in symptoms than these thumbnail sketches allow. If you become ill following a backcountry excursion, tell your doctor you were recently backpacking or hiking. Both Lyme disease and Rocky Mountain spotted fever can be treated with antibiotics.

Bees and Wasps

For most people, a bee or wasp sting is no more than a minor irritant. But if you are allergic, take a treatment kit with you.

Avoiding Leaves of Three

Poison ivy and poison oak both can cause severe, itchy, allergic reactions starting several hours after you brush against their leaves or branches. The growth pattern of the leaves, which are usually shiny, is described in the expression "Leaves of three, let it be."

The distinctive shiny "leaves of three" of poison ivy.

If you may have touched these plants, wash with soap and water. Better yet, try a product called Tecnu Poison Oak n Ivy Cleanser, which has received rave reviews for its ability to remove the irritating chemicals. It can be used before and even after a rash has begun.

Dealing With Weather

Check the forecast before you go—not so you can leave the tent at home "because the weatherman says it's not going to rain," but so you'll know if

Be prepared for weather changes, as is this hiker on the Milford Track in New Zealand.

you should postpone your trip because of dangerous weather.

High mountains can make their own weather; it can snow even in summer. You don't need to plan for every conceivable extreme, but you do need to be aware of the possibilities so you'll be prepared to cope with adverse conditions.

Spring and fall tend to have the most variable conditions, and sometimes the weather *before* your hike can be a factor. On a warm autumn day in New England, we found our trail almost impassable near a mountaintop because snow that had fallen a few days before had turned to ice.

Lightning

The most common dangerous weather you'll encounter is a thunderstorm. Don't take lightning lightly. It kills many people every year, including some hikers.

Hikers can't avoid lightning storms completely, but they can minimize the danger. Lightning is most likely to strike people in exposed places—such as mountain ridges and open meadows. You often can see a storm approaching; if you do, use the time before its arrival to get away from any exposed areas.

Don't think you're safe because there is a big batch of trees across a field. You can be an attractive target if you're the highest object in a 50-foot (15-m) radius. Thick woods are the best option. (If you're near a trailhead, the inside of a hard-topped car is safest of all.)

Hypothermia

The phrase "he froze to death" conjures images of temperatures so cold they turn blood to ice. In reality, just as you can survive surprisingly cold temperatures, you can die of exposure in surprisingly mild temperatures. The key to survival is knowledge and preparedness.

If you are losing heat faster than your body can generate it, you have hypothermia. If this process continues, it can be lethal. And it can happen at temperatures much higher than you'd think. In windy, wet conditions, temperatures in the 40s and 50s (4-15 °C) can be life threatening to the unprepared hiker. When your clothes (especially fibers like cotton) become wet, they lose their insulating power. Meanwhile the wind can whip away the heat your body generates. An actual temperature of 40 degrees Fahrenheit (4 °C) with a 10-mile (16-km)-per-hour wind feels like it's 28 degrees (–2 °C).

The first signs of hypothermia are chills and shivering, followed by tiredness, lethargy, irritability, and low morale. Uncontrollable shivering is a real danger sign. As hypothermia deepens, it is accompanied by a lack of coordination, an inability to think rationally, slurred speech, and finally collapse, coma, and death.

Heat Exhaustion and Heatstroke

At the other extreme, heat can do you in as well. Water is needed for every bodily function from thinking to walking and for keeping the body cool enough to perform these functions.

Exercise generates heat that must be radiated through the skin or counteracted through sweating. High temperatures and high humidity spell trouble for this process. When air temperature approaches 92 degrees Fahrenheit (33 °C)—the temperature of your skin—heat can be dissipated only through the evaporation of sweat, and humid conditions interfere with evaporation.

Two conditions to be alert for are heat exhaustion and heatstroke. Heat exhaustion comes on gradually (over a long day or even several days) and is characterized by tiredness, weakness, and malaise. You feel generally awful but continue to sweat.

Heatstroke is far more dangerous and comes on more quickly, generally in very hot weather. Your breathing becomes short and labored; muscles may feel like they're on fire. It can develop into blurred vision, dizziness, and nausea. You stop sweating—a real danger sign—and your skin becomes dry and its temperature skyrockets. If you reach this point, your body's cooling mechanisms have broken down and you may lose consciousness.

© Robert Llewellyn Photographer

In hot weather, frequent stops to rest and drink water help prevent heat exhaustion and heatstroke.

STAY SAFE IN ANY WEATHER

In Lightning Storms

1. If you're caught in an exposed place, get away from your backpack and its metal parts, stove, and tent poles. Take your sleeping pad with you if you can get it easily. Get away from isolated trees, the bases of cliffs, or other objects that could be lightning targets. Don't forget that bodies of water can conduct electrical charges.

2. Seek shelter in a low point—a depression in the ground or the like. Crouch, rather than lie, to minimize contact with the ground, through which the lightning stroke can travel. Put your foam pad or a daypack that contains no metal under you for insulation.

In Cold and Wet

1. Prevent hypothermia by dressing warmly and staying dry. Snack and drink continually to keep your stove stoked. A warm hat can be one of the lightest, most important items to pack because you can lose so much heat through your head.

2. If you start to shiver, put on more clothes. If you get wet, change into dry clothes. Never take "a little nip" of booze to warm up—while it makes you feel warmer initially, it leads to greater heat loss.

3. Watch for symptoms in your group and take action without delay. The first priorities are shelter and warm clothes, then hot drink and food. In advanced cases, the only resort may be direct transfer of body heat—two people together in the same sleeping bag.

In Heat

1. Carry plenty of water and drink it before you're thirsty—thirst is the first sign of dehydration. If you notice an extra long time between urinations and that your urine is darker than usual, you are dehydrated and need to drink more. Avoid caffeine and alcohol, which switch on your kidneys and increase your fluid loss.

2. If heat exhaustion occurs, get out of the sun, drink fluids, and rest.

3. At the first sign of heatstroke, get into the shade, drink fluids, and rest. In advanced cases, the only way to cool the body may be by pouring water or other fluids on it or immersion in a stream or lake.

Altitude Adjustments

To see some of the most beautiful places, you'll have to hike at higher altitudes than you're accustomed to. As you rise from sea level, the air becomes thinner. At 10,000 feet (3,048 m), there's 30% less oxygen available than there is at sea level, and for most people, breathing is labored, hills seem steeper, and distances feel longer.

Unless you take the time to adjust, you may get altitude sickness. If you go from a lowland home to 7,000 feet (2,134 m) or higher, here are some precautions:

Take a day or two to get acclimatized before undertaking strenuous activity. Then take it easy on the first day's hike upward. You might climb higher during the day, but each night's sleeping spot should be no more than 1,000 feet (305 m) above the night before. For every 3,000-foot (915-m) gain, take a "rest day." Increase your fluid intake and the percentage of carbohydrates in your diet. (Fats and protein require more oxygen to metabolize.)

© Kent & Donna Dannen

When planning a high-altitude hike, allow time for your body to adjust.

COMFORT TIP At high altitudes, try the "rest step" technique: Take smaller steps and with each step uphill, pause momentarily while your back leg is straight and still bearing your weight.

Anyone becomes ill if instantly transported to an altitude higher than her or his threshold for adjustment—but that threshold varies greatly. Neither cardiovascular fitness nor any other factor can predict your susceptibility, but experience will reveal your limitations.

Altitude sickness can take three forms, one of them merely discomfitting, the other two life threatening.

Acute mountain sickness (AMS), by far the most common, can begin as low as 7,000 feet (2,134 m) and becomes common at 9,000 feet (2,743 m) and higher among people who have not taken the time to acclimatize. The symptoms are headache, nausea, dizziness, loss of appetite, and weakness. Any symptoms are a sign to stop and take more time to acclimate. If that doesn't help, a descent of 1,000 to 3,000 feet (305-915 m) will make you feel much better.

If you are susceptible to AMS but still want to hike high in the mountains, ask your physician about drugs that can help your body adjust.

The other two forms of altitude sickness, cerebral edema and pulmonary edema, are defined by a fluid buildup in the brain or lungs. Both can kill. These usually occur at much higher elevations than does AMS. Mountaineering and mountain medicine books cover these threats in detail. When you're ready to tackle tougher high-altitude trails, head for the library before you head for the hills.

SAFETY TIP The sun's burning rays become stronger with elevation—4% per 1,000 feet (305 m)—so compensate by covering up and using sunscreen.

First Aid

Take a course! The Red Cross's first aid courses teach skills that are good to have wherever you are—at home or far into the woods.

Buy a first aid manual and take your own refresher course before each backcountry trip. Keep a one-page instruction sheet with your first aid supplies at all times. Consult the latest backcountry medicine books at your local outdoors store.

Before each trip, you and your companions should think through possible emergencies and discuss what you would do. For example, what if someone is bitten by a poisonous snake? The panicky moment after a bite is not the time to be arguing about the proper first aid or to be reading the label to see how the Extractor works.

Surviving Hunting Season

One colorful fall day a dapper walker in knickers and a Swiss hat spied our neon orange clothing and asked, "Are you out hunting?"

He looked shocked when we replied, "No, but since it's hunting season, we're trying to avoid being shot."

"That's not a bad idea," he said finally as it dawned on him that being a hiker does not exempt one from being on the wrong end of a hunting mishap.

American national parks are closed to hunting, but national forests, national preserves (which are managed by the National Park Service), national wildlife refuges, and state-managed areas are popular hunting grounds. Always check locally on hunting season dates and places.

If you hike during hunting season—and especially deer season—wear as much of the hunter's traditional blaze orange as you can muster. You can buy inexpensive nylon vests and baseball caps at hunting supply stores.

"Never Hike Alone"

If you hike alone, you take a much bigger chance than if you hike with a group. If you get hurt, a hiking partner can administer first aid, go for help, or both. If there are three or four in your party, one can stay with the injured person while others go for help.

But the maxim "never hike alone," which appears on every list of tips for beginners, has been violated by every experienced hiker. Solitude in a wild area is an exhilarating experience. Just the same, don't even think of going solo until you have plenty of experience dealing with unexpected problems on the trail.

Anything Else?

This long lists of "threats" could make you abandon all thoughts of venturing beyond the city limits. You might be thinking that hiking sounds positively dangerous, but nothing could be further from the truth. The natural world is a wonderfully benign, safe, and peaceful place, especially if you go in with the right equipment on your back and the right facts in your head. We feel much safer in the middle of a wilderness than in the middle of a city. For one thing, the farther you are from a road, the farther you tend to be from threats of crime.

Just be careful on your drive to the trailhead, by far the most perilous part of your whole trip!

5

THE BEST PLACES TO HIKE AND BACKPACK

Now that you've broken in those hiking boots, the question is where to go next. The world is literally at your feet, with enticing choices ranging from the spellbinding depths of redrock canyons to the dazzling heights of alpine mountains.

Contemplating your next weekend hike or exotic trek is one of the great pleasures of being a hiker. It's like studying the dessert cart at a fancy French restaurant: Everything looks so good, it's hard to choose. With "so many trails, so little time," you may find yourself planning your life around tasting as many as possible.

A trip to the library or outdoors store will produce enough trail descriptions from books and magazines to get your feet tapping. Clubs and hiking gear stores often present slide shows on hiking trips—great sources of ideas for your destinations list. New friends from your hiking club also will recommend nearby trails for your weekends and describe their favorite faraway trails for your armchair dreaming.

Hiking can add spice to any vacation trip. Say Hawaii and most people think of beaches, but you'll get to peer into a volcano if you research hiking opportunities before you go. Say France and most people think of wine, food, and chateaux, but hiking will take you into the heart of the countryside, to experience the essence of Provence or Brittany.

© Nancy Hoyt Belcher/Photo Network

One of the payoffs of a hiking vacation: getting a glimpse of a volcanic crater in Hawaii.

Closer to home, you can find year-round hiking opportunities in county and state parks, wildlife refuges, and greenways. Most major metropolitan areas have close-in trails through a natural area. Some cities even have paths that lead from the concrete canyons to the wilderness. For example, from New York City's George Washington Bridge you can hop on the Long Path and follow the Hudson River north to the Catskill Mountains' hemlock forests.

No trail near you? Get a detailed county map and head for those country roads marked by dashes instead of solid lines. These dirt or gravel roads are often just like a wide trail, with one-car-per-hour traffic so you can still hike in quiet and solitude.

TRAVEL TIP   If you're ready to expand your hiking horizons but you can't talk friends into accompanying you or feel you don't quite have the experience, contact one of the many organizations, both nonprofit and commercial, that lead trips to the best spots on every continent. They offer camaraderie, guidance on the conditions you'll be facing and equipment you'll need, and a seasoned leader.

Researching Your Trip

Close-to-home hiking gets you in shape for far-off places, but in addition to leg muscles and aerobic capacity, you need to plan carefully. The key to a successful trip away from your own familiar environment is research, research, research!

When should you go? Although it's cold and muddy on your home trails, it could be warm and dry in prime hiking spots in the opposite hemisphere. Study guidebooks on the country you want to visit for information about the best times to go and about concerns such as rainy seasons and "bug" seasons.

For instance, in the United States there's a hiking destination for every month of the year. In March and April the Southwest explodes with bright desert flowers. Redbud and dogwood blooms sprinkle Virginia's Shenandoah National Park in May; the laurel and rhododendron bring every shade of pink to the Smokies in June. The midsummer sun opens the bright blossoms and clears the snows from the high western mountains. In September the aspens run golden streaks through the evergreens in Utah and Colorado. In

Dudley/Seaborg

High in Utah's Wasatch Mountains, wildflowers bloom profusely in midsummer.

October the crimson maples in Massachusetts set the Berkshires on fire. Winter's dry season means fewer mosquitoes on the Florida Trail.

And you need to know when *not* to go so your dream trip doesn't turn into a nightmare. Trails high in the Rockies can still be blocked by deep snow in June. Desert canyon hikes should be scheduled for the dry months to avoid the risk of flash floods from summer thunderstorms. Spring in northeast U.S. mountains means a long mud season, with mucky trails where human tread can easily damage the fragile soil. Hold off on trips to the north woods until midsummer when the insect hordes abate.

Take all the essential equipment even if you're going on a hiking club or adventure travel trip with a leader, because even seasoned experts sometimes goof. On a hiking trip in Norway led by a major adventure travel company, we headed out for a midnight sun picnic on the Arctic Ocean shore. Our leader had packed such delicacies as lingonberry liqueur and Swiss chocolates. But when we started the 3-hour hike back to the road, an icy fog banished the golden light. After groping for hours through thick mists that limited visibility to one yard (0.91 m), it was clear we were hopelessly lost. The leader had packed everything but his compass!

TIPS FOR FAR-FLUNG TRIPS

If you're flying to your backpacking destination, here are some handy hints:

- A large, tough duffel bag can encase your pack and keep straps from getting caught in airport conveyor belts. If you send your pack through unprotected, shorten and tie up straps so they don't hang down and aren't used as handles. Airlines don't know how to deal with backpacks.
- Many internal-frame packs will fit into overhead compartments. If you don't check your pack, the airline can't send it to Timbuktu when you're headed for Kilimanjaro.
- Wearing your hiking books aboard the plane saves packing space.
- Layers of thermal underwear make good substitutes for sweaters and pajamas. They're less bulky and dry faster.

U.S. Destinations

America's crown jewels spread coast to coast in a stunning collection of national parks. Most have extensive and well-marked trail systems, offering spectacular scenery from snow-capped granite peaks to redrock canyons. Their fame can lead to crowds, but those willing to walk the extra steps can avoid the congestion. Even in the most visited spots, tourists generally don't venture more than 1 or 2 miles (1.6 or 3.2 km) from the parking lot.

Ask the park rangers about the "unpopular" sections that have fewer visitors. At Grand Canyon National Park, for example, the North Rim is far less crowded than the South Rim just because it's less accessible to motorists.

In addition to the well-known national parks such as Yellowstone and Yosemite, the National Park Service manages smaller units called national monuments, national historical parks, national seashores, and national recreation areas. Don't ignore these units. They often offer good hiking and even backpacking opportunities. Examples include Colorado National Monument, Point Reyes National Seashore, and C&O Canal National Historic Park.

Several national forests also offer breathtaking hiking opportunities. Many such forests surround national parks and provide much of the same scenery—minus the tourists. One warning, however: Except for designated wilderness or recreation areas, these vast lands are managed for "multiple use," and extractive uses such as logging, grazing, and mining often

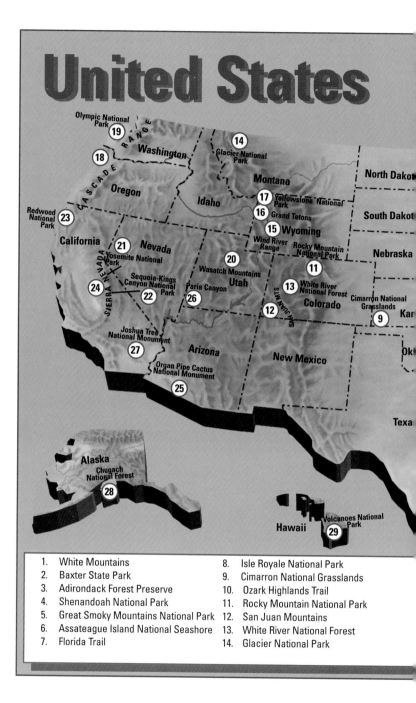

1.	White Mountains	8.	Isle Royale National Park
2.	Baxter State Park	9.	Cimarron National Grasslands
3.	Adirondack Forest Preserve	10.	Ozark Highlands Trail
4.	Shenandoah National Park	11.	Rocky Mountain National Park
5.	Great Smoky Mountains National Park	12.	San Juan Mountains
6.	Assateague Island National Seashore	13.	White River National Forest
7.	Florida Trail	14.	Glacier National Park

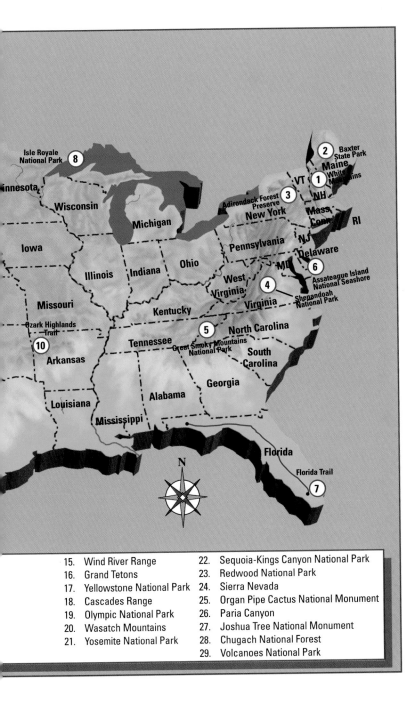

© Robert Hitchman/Photo Network

With a little detective work you can find solitude and beauty in Bureau of Land Management areas.

overshadow recreational uses such as hiking. Logging roads can overlay trails and form nonnavigable mazes. Clear-cuts can reduce the forest to brown dirt and gray stumps and destroy trails. Even sections of the famed Pacific Crest National Scenic Trail have been obliterated.

Much of the land the Bureau of Land Management oversees is desert that ended up in government ownership because it was "the land that nobody wanted." But lying among its 271 million acres (110 million hectares)— nearly one eighth of the United States, in 14 western states—are a host of "undiscovered" hiking gems where you can roam in solitude and pitch your tent wherever you want. No facilities, no rangers, no concessions—but usually no people!

For information on national parks, national forests, and Bureau of Land Management areas, write to the addresses in the appendix. For information on a state's parks and forests, contact the state tourism office. Most states now have 800 numbers; call (800) 555-1212 and ask if the states you're interested in have toll-free numbers.

TRAVEL TIP You can reserve a site at many developed national park campgrounds. Permits are required for backcountry camping in many national parks and wilderness areas. In some jurisdictions, backcountry camping is restricted to designated sites, and reservations are needed at popular times. Check with the local unit for special regulations—preferably before you get there so you won't be disappointed.

THE NORTHEAST

Some of the best hikes in the East are in the White Mountains of New Hampshire. Unlike most eastern mountains where ridgetop trees hide the views until winter, the Whites have rocky ledges and summits from which you can look out on lake-studded valleys and layers of ranges. At lower altitudes, the forest floor is a realm of charm and variety, from insect-catching sundews to ferns, mosses, even orchids. The high ridges, with a tree line of 4,500 to 5,000 feet (1,370 to 1,520 m), harbor plants similar to those in the Arctic.

The Appalachian Trail winds northeast from the Whites through Maine's "100-mile (160-km) wilderness" to its northern terminus on the East's most impressive peak, Mt. Katahdin. Katahdin, with its series of summits connected by the aptly named Knife Edge Trail, is in Baxter State Park. Here you can reserve three-sided shelters a day's hike apart, fall asleep to the magical cry of loons, and wake to the crashings of moose.

The Adirondack Forest Preserve in upstate New York is a huge 6 million–acre (2.4 million–hectare) patchwork of private and public land. Its wilderness is laced with trails that wind past streams and waterfalls and up 4,000-foot (1,220-m) rocky peaks, many with blueberry-covered ledges and exposed summits that provide long views of ranges, valleys, and lakes that mirror the skies.

THE SOUTHEAST

More than 500 miles (800 km) of trails emanate from Skyline Drive in Virginia's Shenandoah National Park. The drive continues south on the Blue Ridge Parkway for 470 miles (756 km)—with more trails along the way—to the premier hiking destination of the Southeast, Great Smoky Mountains National Park. The park straddles the North Carolina-Tennessee border, with misty, luxuriant green mountains, several of them 6,000 feet (1,800 m) high. The mountains are covered in spring with wildflowers, from early lady's slippers and trout lilies to masses of flaming azaleas and purple rhododendrons.

On the Maryland and Virginia border, Assateague Island National Seashore's trail is the sandy shoreline of a barrier island where we've caught glimpses of the famed wild ponies, descendants of the survivors of a shipwrecked Spanish galleon. More than 275 bird species frequent its marshes; peak migration is in September and October.

The Florida Trail offers a perfect winter destination. Its ecosystems range from cypress trees and orchids of subtropical swamps to palm hummocks and rolling pinelands.

THE MIDWEST

The far north lake country is for hikers as well as paddlers and fishers. Michigan's Isle Royale National Park, surrounded by the cobalt waters of Lake Superior, has a rocky, evergreen-studded shoreline and an interior of ridges, swamps, and lakes. Backpackers on the Greenstone Ridge Trail down the island's backbone may hear the rare sound of a howling wolf pack. Midsummer is the best time—after the intense black fly and mosquito season and before the fall chills of late August.

Hikers in Kansas can follow the historic Santa Fe Trail for 22 miles (35 km) through the Cimarron National Grasslands with its vast sweep of sky. More than 280 species of birds come through this stretch of prairie.

© Tim Ernst/Ernst Wilderness

Spring and fall are the best seasons to visit King River Falls in the Arkansas Ozarks.

The Ozark Highlands Trail winds some 190 miles (306 km) through the gentle mountains, hardwood forests, and river bluffs of northwestern Arkansas. Summers are hot, so most hikers head for these hills for the spring wildflowers and the fall colors.

THE WEST

On the exhilarating trails of the Rockies, Cascades, and Sierra Nevada ranges, a typical hike winds from a flowering meadow through evergreens, to a higher and higher series of lakes nestled beneath towering, snow-capped peaks. Because many trailheads are above 8,000 feet (2,440 m), even dayhikers can climb to a high pass or a 13,000-foot (3,960-m) summit and eat lunch while gazing at waves of alpine peaks that extend to the horizon. Midsummer is the best time for this high country.

Visitors to Colorado, the highest state in the country with 54 mountains taller than 14,000 feet (4,270 m), often head for Rocky Mountain National Park. But many of the state's national forests possess similar stunning scenery.

In the cluster of peaks known as the San Juan Mountains, hikers can board the historic narrow-gauge Durango-to-Silverton Railroad and hop off for a 16-mile (25.6-km) overnight backpack into the 11,000-foot (3,350-m) Chicago Basin, which is encircled by majestic peaks.

White River National Forest's trails lead hikers into wilderness areas that boast abundant wildlife, profuse flowers, alpine lakes, rushing streams, scenic peaks, and even a backcountry hot spring.

Midsummer is a good time for llama packing in the Cascades in Washington state.

A list of premier hiking areas of the West could go on forever: Montana's Glacier National Park; Wyoming's Wind River Range, Grand Teton National Park, and Yellowstone National Park; Washington's North Cascades National Park, Olympic National Park, and many national forests; Utah's Wasatch Mountains; and California's Yosemite National Park, Sequoia-Kings Canyon National Park, Redwood National Park, and national forests of the Sierra Nevada.

SAFETY TIP High mountains can generate their own weather, and lightning is a serious danger above timberline. Start early enough to be off exposed ridges by early afternoon. Cumulus clouds piling up are the first sign of an impending storm, but don't be lulled by blue skies overhead when your view westward is restricted. Storms can sneak up from the other side of the mountain.

THE SOUTHWEST

A very different world awaits in the Southwest desert and canyon country. Winter is the best time to hike in Arizona's Organ Pipe Cactus National Monument—through its Sonoran desert, stark mountains, rocky canyons, and dry washes that are home to desert bighorn sheep, mule deer, and collared peccaries. Joshua Tree National Monument east of San Bernardino, California, blooms in early spring, its desert stars and poppies sprinkled among the unique yucca trees.

The beds of rivers that have cut deep canyons through Utah's redrock country provide trails in the spring. Late March is the ideal time to hike Paria Canyon, a 35-mile (56-km) trek through a narrow crevice between vertical ocher walls, fern-lined seeps, and apricot grottoes glowing in the sun. Nearby Escalante Canyon contains cave dwellings, petroglyphs, and natural arches.

SAFETY TIP Water—too much or too little—is always a problem in desert canyon hiking. Plan water sources carefully and be sure to carry enough. Plan to drink at least 4 quarts (3.8 L) on hot days. Check weather forecasts and learn about flash flood dangers.

ALASKA

Hiking opportunities abound in Alaska's vast lands of glaciers, mountains, and tundra where summer's long twilight and midnight sun let you hike as long as your legs hold out. Nearly all of the state is undeveloped and most of it is trailless, so hikers set off cross-country across the sweeping valleys.

Autumn colors and temperatures come early to Alaska's Chugach Mountains.

The 200 miles (320 km) of trails in the Chugach National Forest are a happy exception to the lack of trails. The Kenai Peninsula southeast of Anchorage is one of the most accessible areas. Ranging from sea level to 13,000 feet (3,960 m), it encompasses many of Alaska's special features including glaciers and abundant wildlife: moose, wolves, black bears, grizzly bears, foxes, Dall sheep, mountain goats, beavers, and wolverines.

Mosquitoes also are abundant, so pack netting and insect repellent. The hordes begin to dissipate in August. Be prepared for three seasons. We began one week at Denali National Park in T-shirts, watched the tundra turn from summer green to autumn red, and ended with our tents sagging under a pile of snow.

Any hiking in Alaska calls for special precautions because of grizzly bears. Learn about the dangers before you leave home, then talk to a ranger before setting out.

GOOD TURNS, GOOD FUN

Many hiking opportunities are possible only because of the hard work of volunteers who build and maintain many of our trails. Most local hiking clubs schedule weekend work trips, with après-labor camaraderie and hearty food. Many hikers also opt for vacation "service" trips such as the ones run by the Sierra Club and the American Hiking Society. Groups spend 1 to 2 weeks in spots ranging from Boston's Harbor Islands to California's Trinity Alps, paying little more than their airfare for new muscles, new friends, and a sense of satisfaction. Expenses are tax deductible.

Another type of volunteer trip helps inner-city youths see more than concrete and asphalt. One program is the Miami-based Big City Mountaineers, which combines seasoned adult leaders and young tenderfoots for weeklong backpacking trips in the Rockies.

Canadian Routes

Canada offers an immense variety of hiking and backpacking experiences, from ocean cliffs to glacier-swathed mountains to lush rain forests of firs and ferns. With more than 1 million square miles (2.6 million square km) of wilderness—uncrowded and spectacular—it's a hikers' mecca.

The Canadian Parks Service has offices for five regions: western, prairie and northern, Ontario, Quebec, and Atlantic. The provinces also have park systems. Contact the Canadian Office of Tourism for addresses. For information on hiking in the western mountains, write to the Alpine Club of Canada (the address and phone number are provided in the appendix).

THE ATLANTIC

Quebec's Gaspé Peninsula, Newfoundland's Gros Morne National Park, and Nova Scotia's Cape Breton Island all have maritime-flavored trails, ranging from cobblestone coasts to windswept headlands to high barrens.

Jutting out into the Atlantic on Nova Scotia's northern tip is Cape Breton Highlands National Park, with 27 hiking trails that include a beach path to tidal pools, a boardwalk past orchids and carnivorous bog plants, and trails that climb up through wild roses and pink sheep laurel to 360-degree vistas of the ocean, cliffs, and mountains.

On our favorite route, the Skyline Trail, we hiked out onto a headland 200 feet (60 m) above the Gulf of St. Lawrence where we spotted whales feeding just below our lookout.

Hundred-mile-an-hour (160-km-an-hour) gales rake the highlands and snow falls as late as June, so it's best to savor this island from July through September. French is often spoken in this land of the Acadian settlers.

CENTRAL CANADA

One of Canada's premier hiking routes, the Bruce Trail, winds 468 miles (753 km) along the rocky ridge of Ontario's Niagara Escarpment. Where the trail nears the tip of the Bruce Peninsula, it skirts the tops of white cliffs overlooking the clear, green waters of Georgian Bay. In sheltered grottoes below, dotted with purple harebells and delicate ferns, you can bask in the sun after a swim in the warmer waters off the shallow ledges. If you pitch your tent on the shores of nearby Cyprus Lake, you'll fall asleep to the haunting calls of the loons.

At Point Pelee National Park you can take short but fascinating board-walk trails through a wetland on Lake Erie filled with 700 plant species and, during the spring and fall migrations, up to 300 species of birds. The prime times are May, when the birds pass through in colorful mating plumage, and September, when we saw thousands of migrating Monarch butterflies.

Grasslands National Park on Saskatchewan's vast prairie offers flower-studded native grasses, much the same as when the buffalo roamed. The park is now home to pronghorns, prairie dogs, and badgers.

THE WEST

In the Rockies, Banff, Jasper, Yoho, and Kootenay—the national parks that straddle the Continental Divide—have unforgettable trails. In fact, the entire region could have been aptly named Yoho, which is a Cree word

© Nancy Hoyt Belcher/Photo Network

Exhilarating vistas surround hikers in the Canadian Rockies.

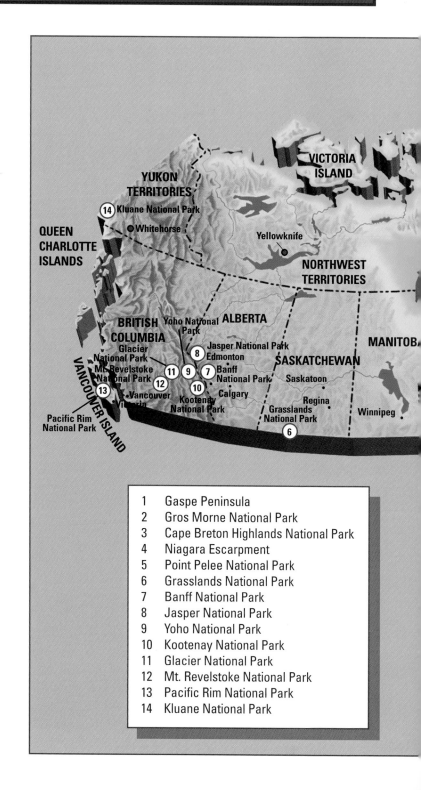

1   Gaspe Peninsula
2   Gros Morne National Park
3   Cape Breton Highlands National Park
4   Niagara Escarpment
5   Point Pelee National Park
6   Grasslands National Park
7   Banff National Park
8   Jasper National Park
9   Yoho National Park
10   Kootenay National Park
11   Glacier National Park
12   Mt. Revelstoke National Park
13   Pacific Rim National Park
14   Kluane National Park

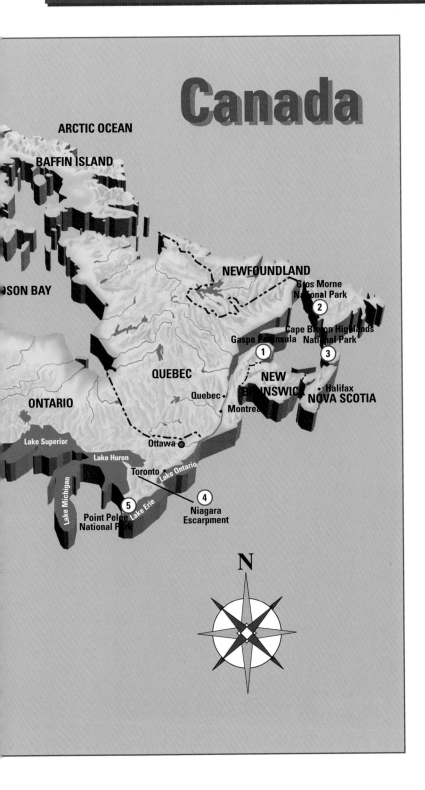

meaning wonder, awe, and amazement.

We hiked to immense glaciers with blue ice caves, bubbling "paint pots," bright flowers in high meadows, and turquoise lakes reflecting the precipitous peaks called the "Canadian Alps." Perhaps our favorite is the trail that leads the hiker past cobalt Moraine Lake, up to flowered meadows and open slopes with a view of all the summits surrounding the famed Valley of the Ten Peaks.

The trails from Lake Louise in Banff National Park are a unique blend of wild and civilized delights. We'd been hiking for 2 miles (3.2 km) up the Lake Agnes Trail when we came upon a "teahouse," a log and stone structure where soup, sandwiches, and desserts were served on a porch with a breathtaking view. When we returned to the lakeside trailhead late in the day, we were met by the strains of a bagpiper strolling by the shores.

In the Selkirks, a rugged mountain range in British Columbia, trails in Glacier National Park lead to panoramic views of glaciers, icefields, and mountains. Nearby Mt. Revelstoke National Park is famed for its alpine flowers—yellow avalanche lilies, red Indian paintbrush, purple lupine.

© Kent & Donna Dannen

Climb to a teahouse or a glacier from Banff National Park's Lake Louise trailhead.

You'll have a good chance of spotting nimble mountain goats on the cliffs above the trails in both parks.

The trails in the Rockies and the Selkirks are snow free and flower strewn from mid-July through August. Grizzlies inhabit the territory; plan accordingly.

At Pacific Rim National Park on Vancouver Island, where the land meets the sea, hikers can take short nature trails through the lush rain forest or explore coves with sea arches and bluffs. A challenging 45-mile (72-km) wilderness trail features sea caves, virgin forests, battered shipwrecks, basking seals, and tidal pools full of bright urchins and starfish.

THE FAR NORTH

The Yukon and the Northwest Territories have few developed trails. This wild, rugged land above the 60th parallel, home to wolves, caribou, Arctic foxes, and even polar bears, is a hiking destination for those with extensive remote wilderness experience and an adventuresome spirit. Kluane National Park, a wilderness half the size of Switzerland, does offer short nature trails off the Alaska Highway and posted day-use trails. Take your warm layers, rain gear, and eyeshades—summer daylight lasts as long as 19 hours.

TRAVEL TIP Most countries use the metric system, in which trail distances are calculated in kilometers and altitudes in meters. To convert kilometers to miles, multiply the number of kilometers by 0.62; to convert miles to kilometers, multiply the number of miles by 1.6. To convert meters to feet, multiply the number of meters by 3.28, and to convert feet to meters, multiply the number of feet by 0.3.

British Pathways

More than 50 long-distance trails in Britain offer landscapes from mountains to moors to pastoral lake country to rocky shorelines. Unlike the United States, British tradition allows strangers to cross private property along established paths, where stiles enable hikers to climb easily over fences and hedgerows. Many trails also have pubs, small hotels, and farmhouse bed-and-breakfasts spaced so hikers of average ability and speed can walk unencumbered for several days.

The Coast to Coast Walk from Saint Bees on the Irish Sea to Robin Hood's Bay on the North Sea is termed by many "the finest walk in Britain," with an exciting diversity of scenery. In its 190 miles (306 km) through the Lake District, the mountains of Cumbria, and the Yorkshire moors, it passes ancient abbeys and villages.

Two long paths follow the jagged western coastline. The longest trail in Britain, the South West Peninsula Coast Path, runs for 500 miles (805 km) from Minehead around Land's End to Poole Harbour. The Pembrokeshire Path's 170 miles (272 km) from St. Dogmael's to Amroth takes hikers past red rock sea cliffs, villages, and 13th-century castles and cathedrals.

Offa's Dyke Path follows the border between England and Wales along the 8th-century earthwork built by King Offa to hold off the Welsh. In the southwest, Pilgrims Way follows the Middle Ages route through Kent from Winchester to Canterbury Cathedral, where Thomas à Becket was martyred in the 12th century. From the Roman spas in Bath, the Cotswold Way follows the steep western edge of the Cotswold hills some 95 miles (152 km) to Campden.

From Scotland's Glasgow, the West Highland Way goes 100 miles (160 km) through the heather, past Loch Lomond, past the granite giant Ben Nevis to Fort William. The last half of the trip is along old military roads.

For information on Britain's trails, contact the British Ramblers' Association (the address and phone number are provided in the appendix).

Expect rain at any time. The odds for a dry day are best in early summer.

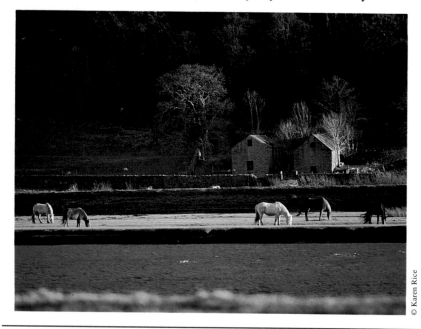

© Karen Rice

Britain offers many landscapes, from mountains to moors to pastoral country.

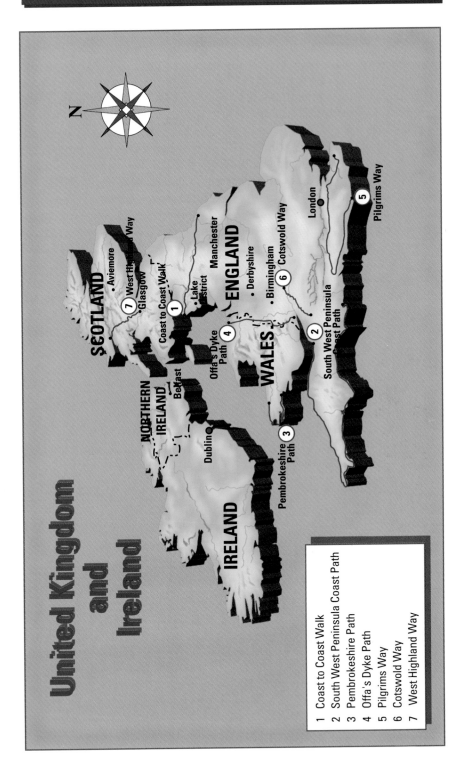

United Kingdom and Ireland

1 Coast to Coast Walk
2 South West Peninsula Coast Path
3 Pembrokeshire Path
4 Offa's Dyke Path
5 Pilgrims Way
6 Cotswold Way
7 West Highland Way

European Trails

Trails and country roads on the European continent offer a fascinating variety of cultures and scenery, from the heights of the Alps to the depths of a Greek gorge. A network of European long-distance footpaths—called E-Paths—cross national frontiers.

The "Haute Route" is a classic trek across the Alps from Chamonix, France, to Zermatt, Switzerland. You can hike it without sleeping bag or tent, staying at village or alpine dormitories. The route passes 10 of the 12 highest peaks in western Europe, including the dazzling, glacier-clad Matterhorn and Mont Blanc.

France has some 18,000 miles (28,970 km) of long-distance trails. One can walk through the Cezanne landscape of the Cévennes, the chateaux country of the Loire, or the vineyards of Burgundy; along the wild Breton seacoast; or past the ancient Roman ruins, small hilltop villages, rocky olive groves, and bustling country markets of Provence.

Between France and Spain, the Pyrenees rise to higher than 11,000 feet (3,350 m) and offer rugged hiking through the Basque country.

In Italy, you can walk through Tuscany among vineyards, monasteries, and Etruscan villages, or hut to hut among the craggy peaks of the Dolomites.

And on the Greek island of Crete is the 13-mile (21-km) Samaria gorge, Europe's longest. The trail starts at about 4,000 feet (1,200 m) and drops between towering walls along a dry river bed, sometimes only 10 feet (3 m) wide, to a seaside village. The gorge is open from May to October, but inquire about conditions at the tourism office in Iráklion before setting off. Flash floods have claimed many lives.

© Chad Ehlers/Photo Network

A typical view in the Swiss Alps, above Lauterbrunnen near Grindenwald.

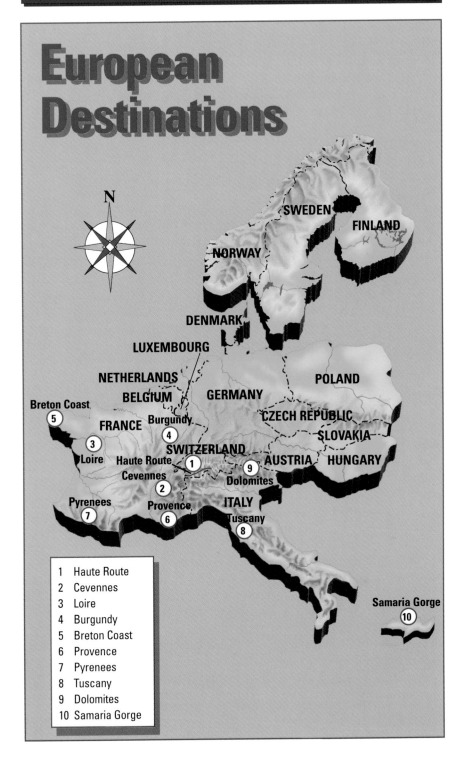

European Destinations

1 Haute Route
2 Cevennes
3 Loire
4 Burgundy
5 Breton Coast
6 Provence
7 Pyrenees
8 Tuscany
9 Dolomites
10 Samaria Gorge

On the continent, the lowlands are lovely from spring through fall. In the Alps, the hiking season extends from the end of June to October. For information, contact the European Ramblers' Association. For information on French trails, contact the Fédération Française de la Randonnée Pédestre. You can make reservations to stay in the Swiss huts through the Schweizer Alpen Club. For information on hiking in the Italian Alps, contact the Club Alpino Italiano (the addresses and phone numbers are provided in the appendix).

TRAVEL TIP Don't plan to camp in the Alps. In an effort to preserve the fragile terrain, camping is discouraged and often prohibited. Hikers stay in high mountain dormitories or mountain inns in little villages. Reservations, which can be made through the alpine club of the country where you'll be hiking, are necessary for weekends and for August, the month when most French and Italians go on vacation.

Trails Down Under

AUSTRALIA

This immense island continent has more than 100 major national parks, with trails through an amazing variety of scenery and wildlife, from the northern tropics to alpine vistas to an island of koalas and kangaroos.

The South Coast Trail on the island of Tasmania offers a trek through button-grass plains, mountains, ocean beaches, cliffs, and coves. In Grampians National Park, the largest in Victoria, hikers may spot koalas or hear the kookaburras "laughing." Kosciusko National Park's trails traverse Australia's most extensive alpine region and pass caves with thermal pools for soothing weary muscles. In Queensland, Lamington National Park's trails through the rain forests offer access to a great bird-watching area. The trails in Kangaroo Island's Flinders Chase National Park traverse the habitat of parrots, kangaroos, and koalas.

Australia's Bicentennial National Trail stretches 3,300 miles (5,310 km) from tropical North Queensland to Victoria, following historic coach routes, bullock trails, and country roads. It links 18 national parks and traverses tropical rain forests, rugged mountains, plains, valleys, and gorges.

Travel is best in Australia's southern sections from October to April and

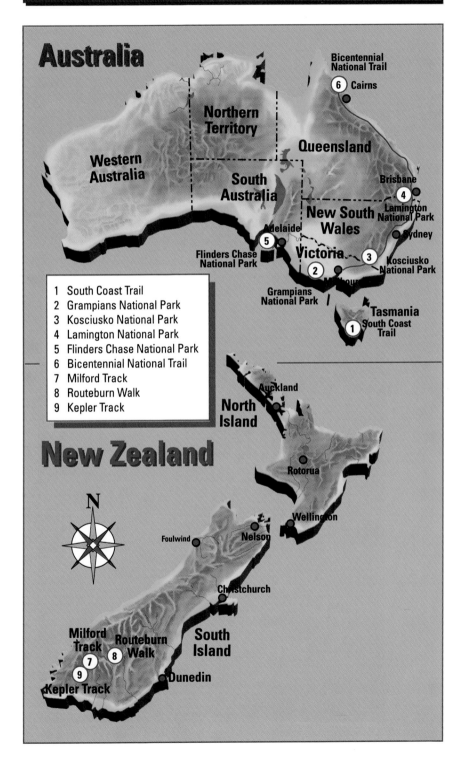

Australia

Western Australia

Northern Territory

Queensland

South Australia

New South Wales

Victoria

Tasmania

Bicentennial National Trail

(6) Cairns

Brisbane

(4)

Lamington National Park

Adelaide

(5)

Flinders Chase National Park

Sydney

(3)

Kosciusko National Park

(2)

Melbourne

Grampians National Park

(1) South Coast Trail

1 South Coast Trail
2 Grampians National Park
3 Kosciusko National Park
4 Lamington National Park
5 Flinders Chase National Park
6 Bicentennial National Trail
7 Milford Track
8 Routeburn Walk
9 Kepler Track

New Zealand

N

Auckland

North Island

Rotorua

Wellington

Foulwind

Nelson

Christchurch

South Island

Milford Track

(7)

Routeburn Walk

(8)

(9)

Kepler Track

Dunedin

in the alpine regions from December to March. Queensland's far north trails are best from May to September. New South Wales has something for every season.

Most states have a federation of bushwalking clubs. For the names and addresses of the federations and major clubs, check the *Lonely Planet Walking Guide: Bushwalking in Australia*. For information on Australia's length-of-the-country trail, contact the Bicentennial National Trail (the address is provided in the appendix).

NEW ZEALAND

The South Island offers a number of trails. The Milford Track is usually on any "top 10 hikes in the world" list. The 33-mile (53-km) trail passes countless waterfalls, precipitous granite walls, craggy peaks with glaciers, and fern forests on its way from the head of Lake Te Anau to Milford Sound in Fiordland National Park. Only 80 trekkers a day are allowed to start on the one-way trail. The groups are staggered, and hikers stop at assigned overnight spots, either rudimentary huts or more expensive dormitories complete with hot showers.

© Blaine Harrington III

The hiking season for New Zealand's Milford Track extends from November to April.

The Routeburn Walk climbs out of river valleys into a high-peaks region with sweeping vistas of snow-capped peaks and deep glacial valleys. The Kepler Track offers a 3-day walk along the backbone of the "Southern Alps."

Take insect repellent to ward off the sand flies. For information on trails, contact The Secretary, New Zealand Walkway Commission (the address is provided in the appendix). *The Lonely Planet Guide: Tramping in New Zealand* lists regional Department of Conservation office addresses.

The Milford Track area averages 300 inches (7.6 m) of rain per year, so take your slicker and a waterproof camera to catch the incredible profusion of waterfalls. The season extends from November to April. For reservations, contact the Tourist Hotel Corporation (P.O. Box 185, Te Anau).

TRAVEL TIP   If you're a visitor from the northern hemisphere, your compass won't work correctly below the equator; buy a new one when you get there or have yours adjusted before you leave.

The Himalayas

No listing of premier hiking areas would be complete without mentioning what many consider the greatest mountain range in the world, the ultimate dream of many a hiker. Despite images the Himalayas conjure of technical climbing on Mt. Everest, treks there are available that reach no higher than

The ultimate dream of many a backpacker: trekking in Nepal.

8,000 feet (2,440 m), in the shadows of 25,000-foot (7,600-m) massifs, combining fascinating cultures with spectacular scenery. It's also possible to make the walk to Everest Base Camp at 18,000 feet (5,490 m).

TRAVEL TIP   Do your homework first. Third World travel requires advance inoculations and special precautions. But before you go to any unfamiliar region or foreign country, make sure you know the facts about everything that could spoil your trip—from monsoons to microbes.

Speaking the Language

A traveler's dictionary is as useful as a guidebook when you travel in another country, but the typical little paperback doesn't include hiking terms.

In French-speaking regions, you'll hike with your fellow "randonneurs" along "sentiers" (trails) over high mountain "cols" (passes), stay in a "refuge" (climbers' dormitory), and descend into a "val" (valley) the next day, perhaps staying at a "gîte d'étape" (an inn or private home) in a hamlet at the head of the valley. Be alert for falling rocks if you see a "chute des pierres" sign.

In German, a footpath is a "fussweg," and a hiking trail is a "wanderweg." Up in the mountains, where "steinshlag" means rockfall warning, a more challenging trail is a "berweg," and one high above a valley is a "hohenweg." A pass may be called a "joch," "sattel," or "furgg." Mountain hikers sleep in simple inns called "berghotels" or alpine "huttes."

An Italian trail is a "sentiero," and a pass is a "passo." A mountain hut is called a "rifugio," "capanna," or "baito." "Caduta di sassi" means "watch out for falling rocks."

In Switzerland, French, German, and Italian are spoken, so you might encounter any of these terms as you move from one region to another.

In the Alps and Dolomites, watch out for what the Germans call "kletterwegs" and the Italians call "via ferrate," which literally means "routes of iron." These terms designate trail sections that traverse sheer walls and narrow ledges where hikers climb metal ladders or cling to protective cables—not fit for people with acrophobia!

If you're from the United States, you won't need any translating aids to travel easily in British Commonwealth countries, but even there you will encounter new hiking terms.

In Great Britain you'll "ramble" along "paths," following the "waymarks" (blazes) up the "fells" (barren hills) and down into the "glens" (mountain valleys). Down under in Australia you'll "bushwalk," and in New Zealand you'll "tramp" along "tracks" (well-defined trails) or "routes" (lightly marked trails).

Hike Infinitum

After you've explored all the regions we've described, there's still so much more. The list never ends: the Inca Trail in Peru, through the "Gates of the Sun" and down to fabled Machu Picchu; the "Avenue of the Volcanoes" in Ecuador; hut to hut in Japan's North Alps; and the isolated Berber villages in Morocco's High Atlas Mountains. There's a world to savor through the intimate journeys taken by those who travel on foot.

© William Mitchell/Photo Network

Visiting another time and culture: Machu Picchu on the Inca Trail in Peru.

6

PURSUING HIKING AND BACKPACKING FURTHER

Al Frost and his brother were teenagers when they set out on their first hiking trip: a 4-day tramp across high desert canyonlands to the Colorado River. "We stuffed our pockets with raisins and cracked wheat. Other than that, we took nothing but the clothes on our backs, a sack of bread and jerky, and an old sawed-off shotgun. We figured that we'd just live off the jackrabbits. Well, the coyotes were so thick that we didn't see a single rabbit." They passed hungry nights curled up next to a fire, waking up to throw on another log when the blaze burned too low.

All the same, it was the beginning of a lifelong love affair with the wilderness, and 60 years later, Al is still exploring the slickrock country.

We asked this expert to show us a route through it for the American Discovery Trail.

One day as we leaned back on our packs and munched dried fruit and trail mix, Al pointed at a pink-and-white toadstool-shaped butte on the other side of Beef Basin and said, "I'm going to have to go there someday. It just looks so interesting, towering over Cataract Canyon like that. I wonder what the view's like." On our 6-day backpack, he explored a canyon new to him, and found two more places he'd "have to go visit." At age 76, his "life list" of "must sees" was still growing on every trip!

It's not hard to understand how hiking can become a lifetime avocation. As the list in chapter 5 shows, there are always more places to go, as your new skills in hiking and backpacking open an entire natural world for your exploration, and many ways to do so.

Dudley/Seaborg © BACKPACKER Magazine

Al Frost, a 76-year-old canyon country guide, leads the American Discovery Trail scouting team through a narrow crevice.

Pack-Free Overnights

The transition from dayhiking to backpacking is a natural progression, but not one that every hiker chooses to make. Many find the weight of a full pack interferes so much with their enjoyment that they prefer to reach their favorite places on dayhikes. But they forego the quiet nights on mountaintops and the prime wildlife viewing times of dawn and dusk.

You can almost have your cake and eat it too if you hike to remote lodges and huts that offer hot meals and a soft bed for overnighters. No electricity, just the soft glow of kerosene lanterns; no television, just the spectacle of a mountain sunset.

There are a few of these places in the United States. LeConte Lodge sits atop the 6,593-foot (2,010-m) eponymous mountain in the heart of Great Smoky Mountains National Park. In Glacier National Park, mountain goats skip around Sperry Chalet's rocks at dusk, and Granite Park Chalet is nestled just under the Continental Divide. You can travel from hut to hut for more than a week in New Hampshire's White Mountains, thanks to a series of lodges run by the Appalachian Mountain Club.

Europe has far more mountain lodges, ranging from Spanish refuges to Norwegian huts. Japan's North Alps offer many hut-to-hut opportunities.

You also can penetrate deep into the wilderness by hiring an outfitter who will pack your gear in on horses, mules, or llamas.

Long-Distance Trails

If you want to see the really remote places, a full backpack is the only way. As you gain experience, your trips can become progressively longer. The weekend trip becomes the weeklong trip, then the 2-week trip, even a month's trip, until, who knows, you could join the growing legion of long-distance hikers.

These hardy people tackle the several-month challenge of the premier long-distance trails. Each year, about 200 people spend 5 months or so covering the Appalachian Trail's 2,100 miles (3,380 km). Others follow the Pacific Crest Trail along the mountains of the U.S. West Coast, from Mexico to Canada. There are now eight European Long-Distance Footpaths that crisscross the continent, from the Atlantic to the Carpathians, from the Baltic to the Mediterranean.

But a long-distance trail experience doesn't have to be a 5-month excursion. You could take 2 or 3 weeks and try the 200-mile (320-km) John Muir Trail through California's Sierra Nevada or the 190-mile (306-km) Coast to Coast Walk across England.

Dudley/Seaborg © BACKPACKER Magazine

After you gain experience and endurance you can venture out on rugged trails to exciting remote destinations.

Many people have hiked the entire Appalachian Trail a piece at a time over many years: a dayhike here, a week's trek there, until they've covered the whole trail. Once signs are up on the 5,000-mile (8,050-km) American Discovery Trail, you can set out to really see the USA, perhaps completing one state each year.

Peak Bagging and High Pointing

Long-distance trails appeal to many hikers who find that aiming at a goal enhances their enjoyment. That is certainly true of "peak baggers," who just love to climb up to where they can look down on everyone else and aren't satisfied until they've climbed—bagged—every peak within view. Some common goals include New Hampshire's forty-eight 4,000-foot (1,219-m) peaks, the Adirondacks' forty-six 4,000-footers, and Colorado's fifty-four 14,000-foot (4,267-m) peaks. Perhaps the most extreme case of this affliction was suffered by Dick Bass and Frank Wells, who attempted to climb the high points of the seven continents in one year.

Some people's goals send them places you've probably never thought of visiting, like White Butte, North Dakota. Recognize that name? A "high pointer" would. These hikers want to reach the high point in each of the 50 states.

Some of the high points are barely noticeable; Delaware's is a bump on a highway. Others can be reached in a dayhike. A few are much more difficult. For instance, Wyoming's Gannett Peak requires a 20-mile (32-km) hike and an 8,500-foot (2,591-m) climb. Peaks like Gannett or Alaska's Mt. McKinley require mountaineering skills.

Mountaineering

Mountaineering simply means climbing mountains for sport, but it implies a higher degree of skill than required for hiking. Many mountains are "technical climbs," and call for use of ropes, rock-climbing skills, and experience on snow, ice, and glaciers.

With some training, it's amazing how many mountains you can climb. The expression "The sky's the limit" can be taken literally.

Neophytes often head to a "snow school" such as the one at Washington state's Mt. Rainier run by Lou Whittaker, leader of the first American expedition up the north face of Mt. Everest. Here, after being outfitted with ice axes and crampons with 12-inch (30-cm) spikes for your plastic mountain boots, you spend a day learning to arrest a slide down an icy slope.

© Eric Sanford/Photo Network

Mountaineering on Island Peak in Nepal.

The next day a guide leads you to the 10,000-foot (3,048-m) base camp. At 1 a.m. on the third day, you set out, roped to your group, across steep snowfields and crevassed glaciers, using the pressure-breathing and rest-step techniques you've been taught. If all goes well, you reach the 14,411-foot (4,392-m) summit 8 hours later.

Snowshoeing and Cross-Country Skiing

Climbing higher and higher is one way to extend your hiking experiences. Another way is to continue through a snow-covered winter. Amid crisp air and bare branches, the vistas are the best of the year. The woods are especially beautiful in their white winter mantle.

If the snow gets too deep to plow through, snowshoes and cross-country skis allow you to skim along the top.

If you can walk, you can snowshoe. Snowshoes require little technique, simply spreading your weight over a greater area. You just need to keep your feet a little farther apart, keep the weight over the balls of your feet going uphill, and lean forward a little going downhill. You won't cover as much ground as you can in summer, however.

© R. Bossi

Snowshoes let you extend your hiking experiences through the winter.

Cross-country skiing requires more technique. The bindings on most flexible, narrow Nordic skis attach to boots at the toe, leaving the heel free for a natural striding motion uphill. You can actually ski uphill almost as fast as you can hike. Then you can zip downhill in a fast, exhilarating ride. With a little instruction and practice, you can become proficient enough to enjoy yourself in the winter woods.

Most backpackers trade their tents for a roof over their heads in snow season—and inn-to-inn and hut-to-hut opportunities exist in winter. But a surprising number like to camp out overnight. With the right layers, tent, and sleeping bag, you can actually be comfortable on a night when the wind is howling and the temperature is zero.

Off-Trail Travel

For some, even the trails are too limiting. When the map shows a lake just over the next ridge, how do you know it's not the most beautiful place in the world unless you go see? If you're proficient with map and compass, you don't need a trail to find out. You simply find your own route to the wildest places, where you won't see another soul or even soleprint. You take another step toward total immersion in the wilderness when you leave behind your last thin link to civilization—the trail.

Off-trail travel is also called going cross-country or bushwhacking. In the United States, it's more enjoyable in the sparsely vegetated, high-elevation western mountains than in eastern forests where heavy growth makes it tough going except in winter.

For some people, a sport is not complete without competition. And hiking can offer various opportunities for that.

These bushwacking hikers have attained total immersion in the wilderness.

Orienteering

We were taking a stroll through the woods one day when we heard a commotion. A man came crashing through the bushes, bumping into trees as he stared at his map and compass. Moments later, another man came sailing over a small cliff face, landing in a heap at its base. He picked himself up, never taking his eyes off his compass, and was off running again. We found out later these two were in an orienteering race.

Orienteering is like a treasure hunt with your map and compass. You're given minimal directions, such as a compass heading and distance, to a checkpoint. At checkpoint 1, you find the instructions to checkpoint 2 and so on through the course.

Orienteering can be an individual challenge or a competitive sport in which participants are timed against each other.

Endurance Hiking and Trail Running

If you are as interested in exercise as in seeing the country, try endurance hiking or trail running. Both can be done on your own or as part of an organized event.

For example, each year our local trail club sponsors a 50-kilometer (30-mile) hike. Check stations along the way offer food, water, and medical help. Most people hike, but some run.

The superfit can enter events such as the annual 100-mile (160-km) run on California's Western States Trail. The run begins near Lake Tahoe and goes over the Sierra crest all the way to the Gold Rush country in the western foothills. Those who finish within 24 hours earn gold belt buckles, a real mark of prestige.

Maintaining Connections

Finally, if trails give you joy, you may decide to give something back by helping maintain them. Trails don't just happen by themselves, and they don't stay there by themselves—erosion, fallen trees, briars, and brambles are constantly attempting a hostile takeover.

Your local trail club's schedule probably includes a combination of hikes and work trips. The Appalachian Trail, for example, was built entirely by volunteers and is maintained by a network of clubs in eastern U.S. cities.

If you like to hike, there's a good chance you'll enjoy trail maintenance. It's outdoors, it's constructive, it's good exercise, and it's sociable. In fact, some hikers get so enthused they spend their weekends working on trails instead of hiking on them!

We maintain a mile (1.6 km) of the Appalachian Trail near our house. The time we spend clipping vegetation keeps us connected to the trail, to the hikers who pass us, and by extension, to all the world's trails and wild places.

That feeling of connectedness is a vital reason for hiking. John Muir said, "Every time we try to pick something out from nature, we find that it is connected to everything else." And when we venture forth in the natural world, we feel connected to everything else.

That thin ribbon of trodden dirt is a connection that leads to a whole world that needs exploring. The trouble is, like Al Frost, every time we walk somewhere, we find two more places we'll "have to go visit."

And the connection stays with us when we return home, manifesting itself as an increased feeling of responsibility for caring for the environment in the way we live. May you find that connection, too. Now that you've got the rudiments, you can take advice from Muir: "Walk away quietly in any direction and taste the freedom of the mountains."

Happy hiking!

© R. Bossi

"Taste the freedom of the mountains": Mt. Jefferson in the White Mountains of New Hampshire.

APPENDIX

FOR MORE INFORMATION

Organizations

United States

American Hiking Society
P.O. Box 20160
Washington, DC 20041
(703) 255-9304

A national membership organization concerned with the interests of hikers and backpackers. Organizes "Volunteer Vacations"—2-week trail maintenance work trips nationwide. AHS does not sponsor hiking trips but maintains a database of local organizations that do. It can help you locate a hiking club near where you live.

Sierra Club
730 Polk St.
San Francisco, CA 94109
(415) 776-2211

> A national environmental organization that sponsors backcountry hiking and service trips in the United States and other countries. Local chapters organize hikes and other outings. Contact the national office for the address of your local chapter.

American Volkssport Association
1001 Pat Booker Rd., Ste. 101
Universal City, TX 78148
(210) 659-2112

> Local chapters sponsor frequent walking events, oriented more to road walking than trails. Good events for beginners to try.

Canada

Alpine Club of Canada
Box 1026
Banff, AB T0L 0C0
(403) 762-4481

> Operates huts in western mountains, information source for trails.

Europe

European Ramblers' Association
Reichstrasse 4
D-6600 Saabrucken
Germany
49 - 681 / 39 00 70

> An association of European "ramblers" organizations, it acts as an information clearinghouse and is working to establish a network of cross-border "European long-distance footpaths."

British Ramblers Association
1/5 Wandsworth Rd.
London SW8 2LJ
(01) 582 6878

> A national lobbying group with local chapters that organize activities such as walks, maintenance work, and social events.

France: Fédération Française de la Randonnée Pédestre Centre d'Information
8, avenue Marceau
F-75008 Paris
(33) 1-47 23 62 32

A national lobbying group that works for the creation of trails and publishes trail descriptions.

Germany: Deutscher Alpenverein
Praterinsel 5
8000 München 22
(49) 89-235 0900

Operates mountain huts, source of trail information and maps.

Austria: Österreichischer Alpenverein
Wilhelm-Greil-Strasse 15
A-6010 Innsbruck
(43) 512-58 41 07

Operates huts, source of trail information.

Spain: Federación Española de Montañismo
Alberto Aguilera 3-4
E-28015 Madrid
34 - 1 / 4 45 13 82

A national federation of clubs promoting long-distance trails, also organizes hikes.

Switzerland: Schweizer Alpen Club or Club Alpin Suisse
Helvetiaplatz 4
3005 Bern
(41) 31-43 36 11

Operates huts in Alps, information source for trails.

Italy: Club Alpino Italiano
Via Ugo Foscola 3
Milan
(39) 2-720 22 557

Operates mountain huts, information source for trails.

Australia and New Zealand

Australian Tourist Commission
Level 3
80 William St.
Woolloomooloo, Sydney, NSW 2011
(02) 360-1111

Official government clearinghouse for general information.

Australian Tourist Commission (U.S. office)
489 Fifth Ave.
31st Floor
New York, NY 10017
(212) 687-6300

(Australian) Bicentennial National Trail
P.O. Box 2235
Toowoomba, QLD 4350

Works to develop and maintain this long-distance trail.

The Secretary
New Zealand Walkway Commission
C/- Department of Conservation
Private Bag
Wellington

Official information source for hiking in New Zealand.

Maps and Other Travel Information

Major U.S. Recreational Land Management Agencies

National Park Service, Department of the Interior, 1849 C St. NW, Rm. 1013, Washington, DC 20240.

U.S. Forest Service, Department of Agriculture, 14th St. and Independence Ave. SW, Washington, DC 20250.

Bureau of Land Management, Department of the Interior, 1849 C St. NW, Washington, DC 20240.

United States

U.S. Geological Survey
Box 25286 Denver Federal Center
Denver, CO 80225
(303) 236-7477

First obtain a state index and catalog to identify particular maps.

Trails Illustrated
P.O. Box 3610
Evergreen, CO 80439
(800) 962-1643

Private publishing company that produces maps of many U.S. parks and other prime hiking areas based on USGS maps.

Canada

Canada Map Office
615 Booth Street
Ottawa, ON K1A 0E9
(613) 952-7000

Great Britain

Ordnance Survey
Romsey Rd.
Southampton SO9 4DH

Australia

Division of National Mapping
Sales Office
P.O. Box 31
Belconnen, ACT 2616

New Zealand

Department of Lands and Survey
Private Bag, Charles Ferguson Building
Bowen St.
Wellington

For information on maps worldwide, see *World Mapping Today* by
R.B. Parry and C.R. Perkins Butterworths, 1987

Magazines

Backpacker
33 E. Minor St.
Emmaus, PA 18098
(215) 967-5171

> A practical magazine filled with tips, how-tos, places to go, and equip-
> ment reviews. Each year one issue includes a "Buyer's Guide" list of
> specifications of available equipment. Published nine times per year.
> Subscriptions $27.

Outside
(Editorial:)
1165 N. Clark St.
Chicago, IL 60610
(312) 951-0990
(Subscriptions:)
Box 54729
Boulder, CO 80322
(800) 678-1131

> A dreamer's book compared with the practicality of *Backpacker*. It
> covers a much broader range of outdoor activity but includes equipment
> reviews and places to go. Classified section contains comprehensive
> listing of commercial trips and outfitters. Monthly. Subscriptions $14.95
> in United States.

Books

In-Depth Backpacking Information

The Complete Walker III by Colin Fletcher
Alfred A. Knopf, 3rd edition, 1984

> Everything you wanted to know and more, in detail, by an entertaining
> writer. 668 pages.

The Backpacker's Handbook by Chris Townsend
Ragged Mountain Press, 1991
   Current and in-depth information. 372 pages.

First Aid

Medicine for the Outdoors by Paul S. Auerbach, M.D.
Little, Brown, 1991. 412 pages.

Wilderness Medicine by William Forgey, M.D.
ICS Books, 3rd edition, 1987. 160 pages.

Medicine for Mountaineering and Other Wilderness Activities by James A.
Wilkerson, M.D.
Mountaineers, 4th ed., 1992. 368 pages.

Map and Compass

Be Expert with Map and Compass by Bjorn Kjellstrom
Scribner's, 1976. 176 pages.

Schools Teaching
Outdoors Skills

National Outdoor Leadership School
Dept. R
288 Main St.
Lander, WY 82520
(307) 332-6873

Outward Bound
Rte. 9D
R 2 Box 280
Garrison, NY 10524
(800) 243-8520

HIKING AND BACKPACKING LINGO

To a nonhiker, "loft" refers to an architectural aspect of a house or barn, and "space blanket" sounds like something used on "Star Trek." Below are terms and their trail meanings.

acclimatization (acclimation)—Getting your body adjusted to a stressful environment, such as high altitude, through gradually increasing exposure.

backcountry—An area where there are no roads, no buildings, no civilization— just trails.

backpack—As a noun, a large pack designed to carry gear for overnight camping; as a verb, to hike wearing a backpack.

balaclava—A three-way knit hat that can be a neck gaiter, a cap, and a facemask.

bearing—A directional sighting taken with a compass.

bivouac—To camp unexpectedly without normal equipment.

blaze—An ax cut or a paint mark on a tree or other object designating a trail.

bushwhacking—Off-trail traveling; term usually is reserved for hiking through thick brush or woods.

cairn—A stack of stones marking a trail, usually across a treeless area.

clevis pin—A metal peg with a lock-ring that holds a pack to an external frame.

contour map—A map that shows elevation differences in the features through the use of contour lines; the number of feet or meters between the lines is specified on the map's key.

crevasse—A crack in a glacier, often very deep.

daypack—A pack large enough to carry all the essentials of backcountry travel minus the overnight camping gear.

declination—The difference (measured in degrees) between the direction a compass points at a certain spot and true north.

DEET—N,N-diethyl-meta-toluamide, the active chemical ingredient in some insect repellents.

down—The fluff growing next to the skin of a waterfowl; it is used for insulation in clothing and sleeping bags.

elevation gain—The difference in the number of feet or meters above sea level between the start of a hike and the destination.

external frame—The external support to which a pack is attached.

fanny pack—The smallest hiking pack, actually a large belt with a pouch attached to it.

fill—Down or polyester insulation.

fire ribbon—An incendiary paste in a tube, used for fire starting.

gaiter—A nylon sheath that attaches to the boot and encircles the lower leg to keep out moisture.

geographic north—See *true north.*

Giardia lamblia—Protozoan occurring in backcountry water sources that causes an intestinal illness called giardiasis.

gorp—Also called trail mix, a mixture of high-energy foods such as raisins, nuts, dried fruit, sunflower seeds, coconut, and M&M's.

hipbelt—A wide padded belt on a pack, designed to take most of the weight off the shoulders.

hyperthermia—Dangerously high core body temperature.

hypothermia—Dangerously low core body temperature.

internal frame—Metal stays built into a backpack to provide support for carrying large loads.

loft—The height to which a sleeping bag fluffs when shaken out.

lumbar pack—A pack larger than a fanny pack, worn against the small of the back.

magnetic north—A spot in northern Canada toward which the red needle of a compass points.

moleskin—A protective skin padding that is soft on one side, sticky on the other.

mummy—The warmest shape for a sleeping bag, similar to the Egyptian mummy.

pass—A notch, gap, low point on a ridge, or low point between two mountains.

planimetric map—A map that shows features such as roads, trails, and mountains but without contour lines showing elevation changes.

poncho—A large waterproof rectangle of coated nylon with a hood and a hole for the head.

priming—Pressurizing a stove's fuel tank by pumping air into it, forcing fuel to the burner.

quad or quadrangle—A kind of contour map published by the U.S. Geological Survey.

rain fly—A separate waterproof piece of nylon that fits over a tent's supporting framework.

rucksack—A large knapsack, usually without either an internal or external frame.

scree—Small, loose rock covering a slope.

seam sealing—Applying a waterproofing coating to the stitching holes on the seams of a tent or garment.

shelter—A roofed structure, usually three-sided, for backpackers' overnights.

space blanket—A windproof, waterproof, ultralight, aluminized mylar sheet, usually reflective silver on one side and bright orange on the other.

stuff sacks—Nylon bags of various sizes with drawstring closures.

switchbacks—The zigzags a trail follows up a steep slope to reduce the grade of the climb.

talus—Large rock debris on a slope.

tarp (tarpaulin)—A large sheet of water-repellent material, usually with grommeted holes for ropes.

topo or topographic map—A map with contour elevation lines.

trailhead—The spot on a road where you pick up a trail. It usually has a trail sign.

tree line—The altitude on a mountain above which trees cannot grow.

true north—The direction toward the north pole. Most maps are oriented to it.

watercourse—A constant stream or a channel where water drains after a rain.

white gas—A specially formulated camp stove fuel, available at hardware stores or outdoors shops.

INDEX

ABOUT THE AUTHORS

Dudley/Seaborg © BACKPACKER magazine

Ellen Dudley and Eric Seaborg

Eric Seaborg and Ellen Dudley are the two hiking and backpacking experts recruited to scout the route for the country's first ocean-to-ocean trail. This modern-day Lewis and Clark team spent 14 months exploring the American Discovery Trail's 4,800-mile path from the Pacific to the Atlantic Ocean. For scouting this first transcontinental trail, they were honored by President Bush at the White House and received the 1991 "Enjoy Outdoors America Award."

Eric Seaborg is a long-time trails activist, whose experience ranges from testifying before Congress on trails legislation to building and restoring trails as a backcountry ranger at Washington's Olympic National Park.

Eric was president of the American Hiking Society (AHS) for 3 years and a member of the AHS Board of Directors for 6 years. As AHS president, he was a leader in the last successful campaign to amend the National Trails System Act, which resulted in legislation that significantly boosted the number of trails in the United States. He is a member of the Potomac Appalachian Trail Club (PATC) and the AHS, serves on the AHS advisory board, and as a volunteer maintains a mile of the famous Appalachian Trail.

Eric has contributed many articles on hiking and the outdoors for a variety of publications, including the *Washington Post, Cleveland Plain Dealer, Sierra, Backpacker, American Hiker, National Parks, Events USA, Resort and Travel,* and *Recreation News.* He was also the first editor of *Pathways Across America,* a joint publication on long-distance trails by the National Park Service and the AHS.

Ellen Dudley has been hiking and backpacking for 20 years. As a Girl Scout leader she introduced 7- to 17-year-olds to hiking in the woods. In addition to hiking and backpacking throughout the U.S., she has explored trails in Canada, Peru, Norway, and the French and Swiss Alps. Ellen, a 50-year-old grandmother, is living proof that anyone can enjoy hiking and backpacking.

Ellen is a member of the Sierra Club, AHS, and PATC. For several years she covered environmental issues as a magazine editor and media director. She was editor of *Pathways Across America* and program director for the "Trails for All Americans" project. She has written articles and op-eds on trail-related topics for a number of major newspapers.

Acknowledgments

Pages **65, 78, 128, 131**: © Robert Bossi, Portsmouth, NH

Page **18:** Recreational Equipment, Inc. (REI)

Equipment on pages **12, 19, 24** (backpack, left), **26, 27** (tents, middle and lower photos), **32, 33, 39, 58, 59** courtesy of WildCountry, Inc., Champaign, IL

Equipment on pages **24** (backpack, right) and **27** (tent, upper photo) courtesy of Champaign Surplus Store, Champaign, IL

Models in exercise section: Guy Tieman, Marci D. Herges

The authors gratefully acknowledge Carol Blattspieler of the University Orthopaedics Sports Medicine Center in Colchester, VT, for her assistance with the section on exercises.